Learning

Image retouch
with Photoshop CS6

with 100 practical exercises

Learning
Image retouch with Photoshop CS6
with 100 practical exercises

www.mcb-press.com

Learning Image Retouch with Photoshop CS6 with 100 practical exercises

Copyright © 2013 **MEDIAactive**

First edition: 2013

Published by © **MCB Press** owned by Marcombo. Distributed in USA and Canada by ATLAS BOOKS, 30 Amberwood Parkway, Ashland, Ohio 44805. To contact a representative, please e-mail us at order@bookmasters.com.

www.mcb-press.com

Cover Designer: Ndenu

ISBN: 978-84-267-1831-0

Deposito legal: B-7121-2013

Printed by Publidisa

Introduction

LEARNING IMAGE RETOUCH WITH PHOTOSHOP CS6 WITH 100 PRACTICAL EXERCISES

This book consists of 100 practical exercises that serve as a guide to understand the main functions of the program. Since it is impossible to talk about all the photo retouching features of Photoshop CS6 within this book, we have chosen the most interesting and used ones. After finishing the 100 exercises, the reader will be able to use the multiple tools and functions of the program properly in order to improve the appearance of the digital images.

THE WAY TO LEARN

Our experience in the field of education has led us to design this manual, in which every function is learned by carrying out a practical exercise. The exercises are explained step by step and click by click, to leave no doubts in the execution of the process. In addition, the exercises are illustrated with descriptive images of the most important steps or the results that should be obtained, and also with IMPORTANT boxes that provide further information on each of the topics covered in the exercises.

This system ensures that upon completion of the 100 exercises that make up the manual, the user will be able to cope comfortably with the basic tools of Photoshop CS6 and take advantage of its many benefits.

FILES REQUIRED

If you want to use the sample files that appear in this book, they can be downloaded from www.marcombo.com.

WHO SHOULD READ THIS MANUAL

If you are starting to practice and work with Photoshop, these pages will provide you with a complete guide explaining the main functions, which were specifically designed to improve the appearance and the quality of your photographs. But if you are an expert in the program, it will also be very useful in order to get to know some of the more advanced features.

Each exercise is treated independently, so it is not necessary that you realize them in sequence, although we recommend it, since we have tried to group these exercises thematically. Thus, if you want to address a specific issue, you can go directly to the exercise which deals with this.

THE IMAGE RETOUCH WITH PHOTOSHOP CS6

Among the professional world of photography and the editing of images, one of the most widely distributed and used application is Adobe Photoshop. This manual uses the CS6 version of this program, which is included in the suite Creative Studio CS6, and was especially designed for retouching digital photographs.

In this book, the lessons are dedicated to the retouching and correction of all image types. Besides this, you can create spectacular special effects by applying a combination of different filters and adjustments to the image. Image editing is an artistic endeavor, since it is the user (or client) who chooses the look of your digital photos. If you do not have any advanced knowledge of photography, your images often display problems of overexposure, underexposure, noise, blur, etc. But you cannot only solve these types of failures, but also retouch any type of "physical flaw" (such as acne, freckles, wrinkles etc.) using different techniques, some of which are explained within this manual.

How "**Learning...**" books work...

The title of each exercise concisely expresses what it is about. Thus, if you are interested, you can go directly to the action you want to learn or review.

The exercises have been written systematically step-by-step, so that you will never encounter problems when carrying them out.

The number to the right of the page clearly indicates which exercise you are in.

Important boxes include actions that need to be completed in order to ensure that you perform the exercise correctly. They also contain information that is interesting to learn as it will facilitate your work with the program.

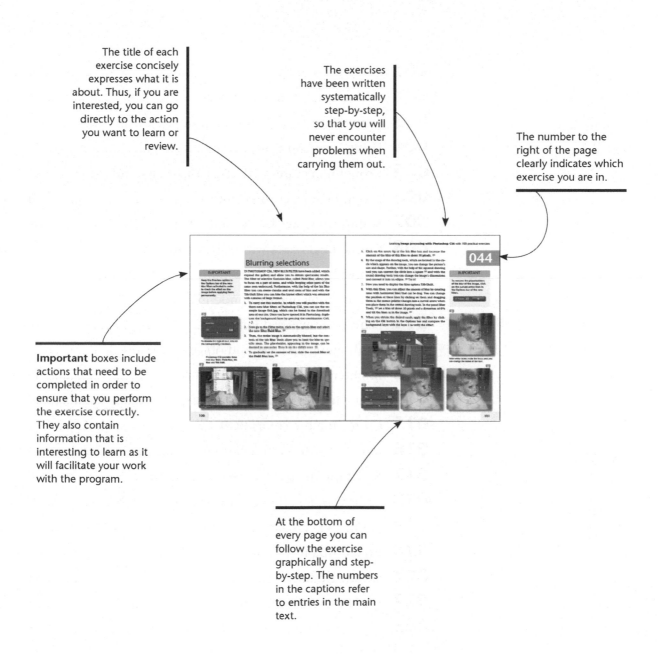

At the bottom of every page you can follow the exercise graphically and step-by-step. The numbers in the captions refer to entries in the main text.

Table of contents

Table of contents

Resizing an image

DIGITAL CAMERAS TEND TO PRODUCE large images even with a resolution that could be considered low in comparison to its size. The resolution, which is normally set at 72 ppi (pixels per inch), is sufficient if the images are to be viewed on a computer screen, but insufficient if you want to obtain hard copies via ink jet or laser printers. With Photoshop it's possible to reduce the size of a photograph while at the same time increasing its resolution and maintaining the picture quality.

1. We recommend using a photograph that fulfills the characteristics mentioned in the introduction. (You can use the example image **001.jpg**.) Open your Photoshop workspace and choose an image you would like to resize.

2. Go to the **Image** menu and select **Image Size**.

3. In the dialog box **Image Size** you can find the image's dimensions and resolution. Make sure that you really want to change the resolution of an image because changes could cause the image to become out of focus, blurred, or pixelated. This effect is caused by an automatic function of the program called resampling of the image, which sometimes changes the dimensions disproportionally to its resolution. Therefore, be-

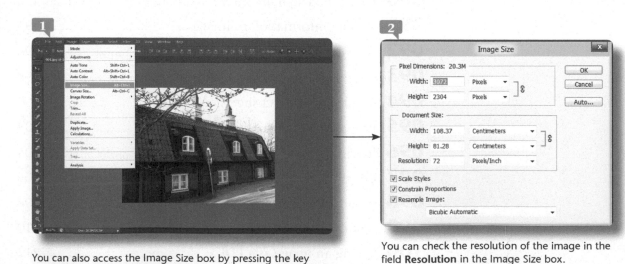

You can also access the Image Size box by pressing the key combination **Alt + Ctrl + I**.

You can check the resolution of the image in the field **Resolution** in the Image Size box.

fore you continue, deselect **Resample Image** by clicking on its checkbox. ▣ This is how you can avoid the loss of the image's quality.

4. Now you can change the resolution value. In this example, and always thinking that our purpose is to print the image on paper, double-click the **Resolution** field and enter the value **150**. ▣

5. You have decreased the dimensions of the image proportionally while achieving a higher resolution. Be aware of the fact that you could still gain a little more resolution if the target of the photograph was a press printer, any further action would reduce the size of the image while mantaining its quality. Click **OK** to accept the process.

6. Apparently there hasn't been any changes made to the image, so you should print it to check the quality. If it is okay, you may return to the Image Size dialog box and keep the **Resample Image** check box enabled: the loss of the quality will be visible on the photograph as you apply all changes.

001

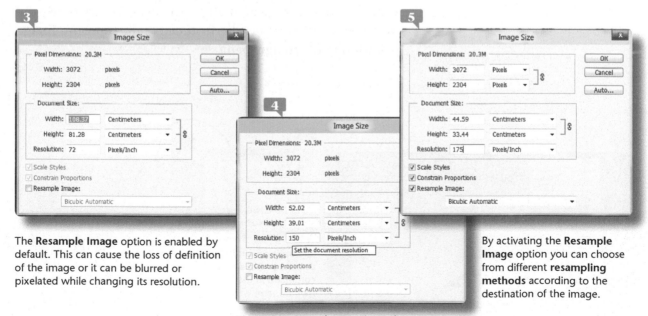

The **Resample Image** option is enabled by default. This can cause the loss of definition of the image or it can be blurred or pixelated while changing its resolution.

The appropriate value to print a photo on an inkjet color printer is **150 pixels per inch**.

By activating the **Resample Image** option you can choose from different **resampling methods** according to the destination of the image.

Tilting and rotating an image

THE IMAGE ROTATION COMMAND, which can be found in the Image menu, can quickly change the orientation of an image or apply a specific degree of inclination. If you want to rotate the entire image a half turn or quarter turn, use the options 180° or 90° to the left or to the right. In order to apply a specific tilt angle it is necessary to use the Arbitrary option.

1. In this exercise you will learn how to rotate and tilt an image with Photoshop. This is a simple command, which can be found in the **Image** menu. To begin, open the image you would like to rotate in the program. (If you like, you can use the sample image **002.jpg**.)

2. Rotate the image 90° clockwise. To do this, open the **Image** menu, then click on the Image Rotation option and choose the **90° CW** command. 1

3. If you work with the sample image, you can see that its orientation has now changed 90° to the right. Depending on the orientation of the image you use, you may need to use the **90° CCW** command to rotate it 90° to the left. Now try to use the **180°** command, which is also included in the submenu **Image Rotation** in the **Image** menu. 2

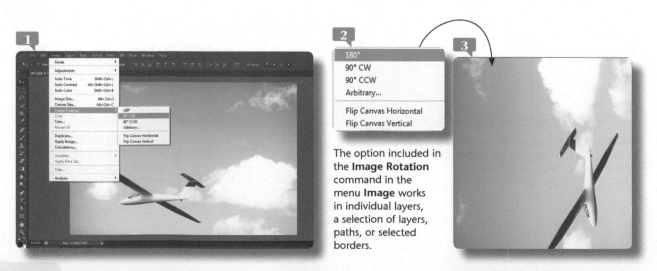

The option included in the **Image Rotation** command in the menu **Image** works in individual layers, a selection of layers, paths, or selected borders.

002

4. Now, the image is facing left. 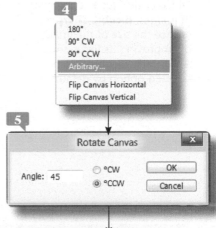 To display the image in its correct orientation again, open the **Image** menu, go to **Image Rotation** and click on the **90° CW** command.

5. Now let's see how to apply a particular pitch to an image. Open the **Image** menu, click on the **Image Rotation** option and select **Arbitrary**.

6. This opens the **Rotate Canvas** dialog box, which you will use to set the angle of inclination you want to apply to the image and apply it to the left or right. In the field **Angle** you need to enter a value between 0 and 359.99. For example, type the value **45** and click on the **°CCW** option.

7. Thus, after accepting the command, the image is inclined 45 degrees to the left. Then press **OK**.

Note that if you want to rotate or tilt specific parts or layers of the image, you should use the **Rotate** option, which can be found in the **Edit** menu and then by clicking on **Transform** in the sub-menu. Further, you can use the angled drawing tools, which appear on the element when selecting it, with the tool **Free Transform**, which is also included in the **Edition** menu. In addition, to gently rotate the canvas and to get a non-destructive view from any angle, you can use the **Rotate View** tool, which can be found under **Hand** in the Tools panel. (This feature requires you to enable drawing OpenGL in the Photoshop preferences).

IMPORTANT

The options **Flip Canvas Horizontal** and **Flip Canvas Vertical** are used to flip an image horizontally or vertically along an axis.

In order to transform an image freely, you must convert Background layer to Layer 0 prior to moving any layer, which is an option in the context menu of the layer in the **Layers** panel.

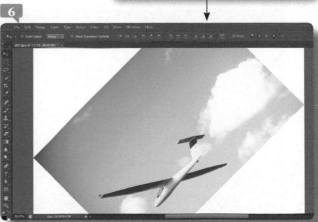

You can restore the original appearance of the image from the **History** panel, which can be displayed in the **Windows** menu, or by closing the file without saving the changes.

Converting a picture into a poster

IMPORTANT

Photoshop uses six interpolation methods to resample images: **Nearest Neighbor** to preserve hard edges and to produce smaller files, **Bilinear** to produce medium-quality files, **Bicubic** to achieve smoother tonal gradations, **Bicubic Smoother**, which is ideal for enlargements of images, **Bicubic Sharper** to reduce the size of the image by improving its focus and, **Automatic Bicubic** which is the selected option by default.

THE CHANGE IN SIZE OF AN IMAGE is directly related to its loss of quality, more specifically, when we increase the size of an image, the quality is reduced. Whereas if you reduce the size of an image, its quality is not affected much, but when you increase the size significantly, an image can become out of focus, blurred, or pixelated. Photoshop can convert normal images into printable poster sizes without losing even one pixel of the image quality.

1. To begin this exercise, open the image you want to enlarge to poster size, go to the **Image menu** and click on the **Image Size** option.

2. In a previous exercise you already had the opportunity to check if the picture has the correct image dimensions and resolution. Enable the **Resample Image** option. [1]

3. Then, open the field under the **Resample Image** option, which by default displays the **Bicubic Automatic** resampling method, and choose **Bicubic Smoother (best for enlargement)**. [2]

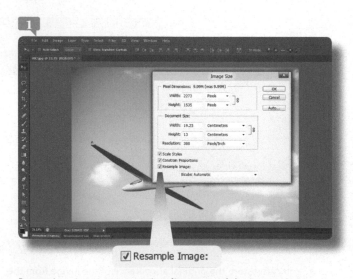

☑ Resample Image:

Remember that the automatic adjustment of the image size in proportion to the set resolution depends on the activation of the **Resample Image** option.

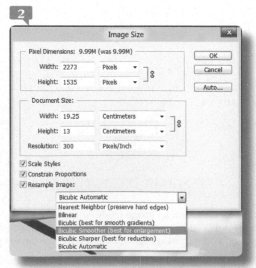

003

4. Then, in the **Width** field of the **Document Size** change the unit **Centimeters** (or the unit you are using right now) to **Percent**.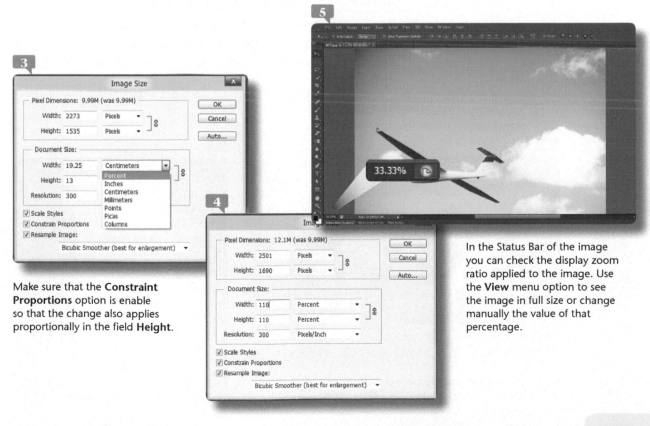

5. The reason for this change is that if you increase the image size by a percentage, then there is absolutely no loss of quality, whereas you increase the size values for width and height, this will cause the already mentioned effects of blur and fade. Therefore, type in the **Width** field the value of **110** and accept the changes.

6. At this point you should repeat this process about ten times according to the initial image size and the poster size you wish to obtain. To do this, you have two options: either repeat the steps mentioned above as many times as you wish or create an action, which with just one button automatically resizes the image. (If you want to create an action, see the exercise in this manual on how to do it.) After changing the size of the image, which previously was a simple picture and now is a poster size, the image now has only a negligible loss of quality.

Make sure that the **Constraint Proportions** option is enable so that the change also applies proportionally in the field **Height**.

In the Status Bar of the image you can check the display zoom ratio applied to the image. Use the **View** menu option to see the image in full size or change manually the value of that percentage.

Using the Crop Tool

CUTTING A PICTURE IS NOT THE SAME as reducing its size, since in the second case the file dimensions are modified without affecting the content and in the first case the areas of the image are discarded. In Photoshop, there are different methods to crop images: defining the content manually with the Crop Tool, indicating the crop size and, form automatically.

1. You can use the sample image **004.jpg** or any other image you want to crop. After opening the image in Photoshop, select the **Crop** Tool, which is the fifth tool on the Tools panel. [1]

2. In Photoshop CS6, this tool has been noticeably improved: now, when you click on the image it shows you a tag with the actual size of the crop area and a practical guide for easier operation. When you have decided which part of the image you want to crop, use the drawing tool in the corners and on the sides of the grid to frame the crop area. [2]

3. In the Options Bar in the **Crop Tool** you can choose between different types of cuts. **Original Ratio** is enabled by default. Pull down this menu and have a look at the available options. [3]

Notice that you can find the name of the layer you are working on while using the crop mode in the **Layers** panel.

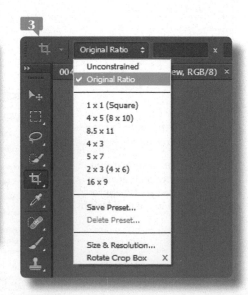

4. You can choose between different sizes of the predetermined cut or choose your own size by using **Save Preset**, change the size and resolution, and rotate the crop box. Keep **Original Ratio** selected and click on the icon that shows a check mark in the Options Bar and see the crop. ▶

5. Taking advantage of the fact that we have not saved the changes yet, you can reestablish the initial appearance of the image. Open the **Edit** menu, and choose **Step Backward**. ▶

6. Let's say you want to achieve an image with the size of 10 × 15 cm. Enter the values **10 cm** and **15 cm** in the fields, where you can customize the size in the Options Bar, ▶ and move the image to the center of the crop area.

7. Before cutting the image, open the field **View** in the Options Bar of the **Crop Tool** in order to check which different display options are available and enabled such as the **Grid** option. ▶

8. Depending on the image and type of cut you want to obtain, one display mode can be more useful than the other. To continue with the cutting, click on the check mark in the Options Bar. If you are satisfied with the result, save the image.

004

IMPORTANT

You can also use the Crop Tool to straighten images while cutting. To do this, select the **Straighten** option in the Options Bar of the tool and draw a straight line on the image to straighten it automatically.

You can also accept the cut of the image by pressing the **Return** button.

You can reestablish the original appearance of the crop box by clicking on the icon that shows a curved arrow in the options bar of the Crop Tool.

Undo Crop	Ctrl+Z
Step Forward	Shift+Ctrl+Z
Step Backward	Alt+Ctrl+Z
Fade...	Shift+Ctrl+F

Cropping pictures with the Crop command

WHEN PRECISION IS NOT NECESSARY while cutting an image (for example to create a collage of images), you can quickly and easily perform the operation without using the Crop Tool with its drawing tools and options. Let us examine how to do it.

1. After opening the image you want to modify in Photoshop (if you wish you can use the sample image **005.jpg**, which can be found in the download area of our website), select the **Rectangular Marquee** tool, which is the second in the Tools panel (you can also select it by pressing the **M** key).

2. By using the drag technique, create a selection rectangle in the area you would like to crop (do not include the area you would like to cut out in this selection area).

3. Go to the **Image** menu and then click on the **Crop** option.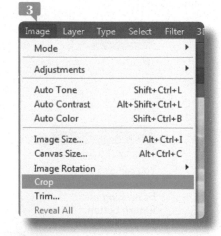

4. The image will automatically be cropped according to your selection. Press the key combination **Ctrl + D** to delete the selection.

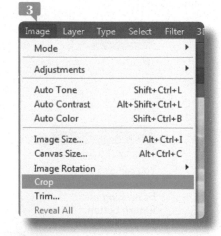

Remember that **you can move the crop area or the select area** you want to define with the help of the dragging technique, by using the mouse or the arrow keys on your keyboard.

New in Photoshop CS6 is the **Label**, which shows you the dimensions of the crop or selected area while selecting and cropping images.

005

5. Photoshop has another way for you to crop an image without using the **Crop** Tool. Instead use the function **Trim**, which is very convenient for cropping, for example, images with white backgrounds (you can use image **005b.jpg**). Open the **Image** menu and click on the **Trim** option. 5

6. In the **Trim Away** section of the dialog box, you need to indicate where you want to make the cut, since by default all sides have been selected (**Top**, **Bottom**, **Left**, and **Right**). Within the section **Based On** you need to specify the color you want to have separated. In this case, enable the **Top Left Pixel Color** option. 6

7. Press **OK** and see how the image is cropped closely without deleting any colored pixels. 7

8. Save the images in Photoshop's own format (PSD) within your image folder and close them.

The **Transparent Pixels** option is only activated when the background image is transparent. This option allows you to cut the transparency of the image edges while leaving the smaller image without transparent pixels.

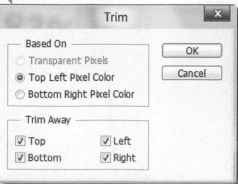

Cropping images in perspective

PHOTOSHOP CS6 HAS ADDED A NEW crop tool called Perspective Crop, with which you can solve problems of distortion in images of, for example, tall buildings or other panoramic perspectives. As you will see in this exercise, operating this tool is simple and helps you to automatically obtain a perfect crop.

1. To perform this exercise, you can use sample image **006.jpg**, which can be found in the download area of our website. Once you have opened the image in Photoshop, press and hold the **Crop Tool** and select the **Perspective Crop Tool.**

2. Once you have activated the tool, create, with the help of the dragging technique, a cropping rectangle on the image so that the graduated rulers can be displayed. (The size of the rectangle does not matter, since you will edit its points in the following steps.)

3. Check that you can hide the grid of the frame crop by disabling the **Show Grid** option in the Options Bar in the Tools panel.

As you can see, all Photoshop cutting tools can also be activated by pressing the **C** key.

4. Now you need to move the drawing tools of the cropping rectangle to adjust the crop to the area you are interested in. Adjust it so that the cropping rectangle stays approximate as in the image. 🔲

5. To continue with the cut in perspective, press the **Return** key or the validation icon in the Options Bar of the Tools panel.

6. Photoshop automatically carries out the cut and shows you the adjusted image as an almost perfect vertical inclination, which in photography can be used to correct possible distortions caused by the perspective. Open the menu, go to **View** and click on the **Rulers** option to display the rulers. 🔲

7. Click on the vertical ruler and, without releasing the button of the mouse, drag a ruler to the image to check if the program has placed the image vertically. 🔲

8. Save the image in Photoshop's own format in your image folder.

New in Photoshop CS6 is that while editing the crop box, a tag will appear next to the edit cursor, which indicates the **degrees of rotation** and the dimensions of the box.

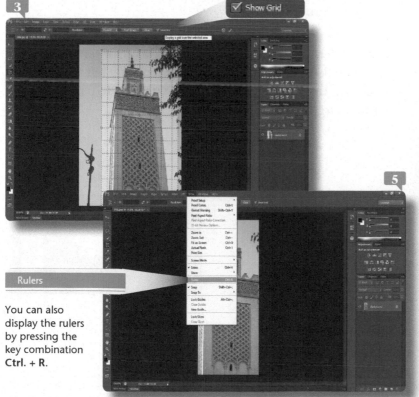

Rulers

You can also display the rulers by pressing the key combination **Ctrl. + R.**

Scaling an image by its content

PHOTOSHOP OFFERS AN INTERESTING FEATURE that allows you to apply a scale based on the content, which reconstructs automatically an image while resizing it. With this new feature you can preserve the most important areas as the image adapts to its new dimensions, so that you will not waste precious time while cropping and touching it up.

1. In this exercise you are going to learn how to use the **Content-Aware Scale**, which can give you panoramic image dimensions without making other adjustments. This time you are going to practice with example image **007.jpg**, which, as always, can be found in the download area on our website. To begin, select the rectangular selection tool in the **Tools** panel and mark a selection rectangle that covers the image without the white background. 🔳

2. Then go to the **Edit** menu and click on the **Content-Aware Scale** option. 🔳

3. In the margins of the image a drawing tool is going to appear, which helps you to modify your horizontal and vertical scale. Click on the center drawing tool on the left and without releasing the mouse button; drag it to the left to cover the white margin on that side. 🔳

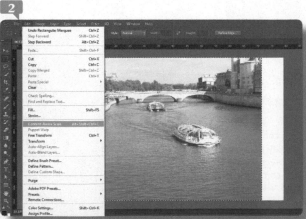

007

4. As you can see, the image will automatically reconstruct itself as you change its width while keeping it in perfect condition and maintaining the proportion of the major areas. As always it is possible to change the scale by applying new values in the **Options Bar** of the Tool panel when working with transformation tools. In this case, besides the values height, width, and position of the image, you can also define in the field **Amount** the threshold for the scale based on the content in order to minimize distortion by selecting a channel to specify which areas you want to protect. Now using the center drawing tool on the right, click and drag until the canvas is completely covered.

5. As a last step, in order to correct the distortion that occurs on the houses on the right side of the image, reduce the value of the field **Amount** in the **Options Bar** to about 50% and apply the scale by clicking on the check mark.

Although a normal scale equally affects all pixels in an image while resizing it, the image could get distorted or deformed by the scale if it includes unimportant visual content. For example, if your photo has a beach background and people are walking along the shore, you can scale the pixels of the water and the sand, whereas the people will not deform.

Use the **Content-Aware Scale** feature to increase or decrease the size of your images without distortions or without having to crop them to improve the result.

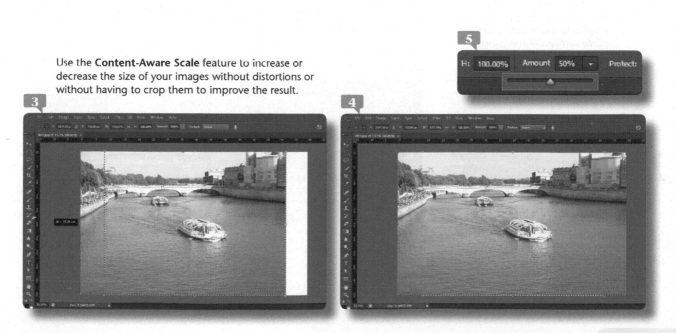

Correcting images with too much flash

USING A FLASH IN PHOTOGRAPHY does not always produce good results if you do not take certain factors into account while taking the picture: overexposure or lack of light in close-ups, shadows, refulgence, etc.. Typical problems resulting from a mis-use of the flash, which are reflected in the images, can later be corrected in Photoshop.

1. In this lesson, we will show you how you can solve the problem of overexposed flash pictures in close-ups. Now, if you do not have a flash problem in the photo you are working with, use example image **008.jpg**. In the **Layers** panel you can see that the image is formed by a single layer called **Background,** and which is locked by default and cannot be changed. Click on that layer and, without releasing the mouse button, drag it to the icon called **Create a new layer** on the bottom of the panel.

2. In this way, you have created a new layer that is identical to the Background layer and which is called **Background copy** (make sure that the new layer is selected in the panel).  Display the field layer blending options, in which the **Normal** option is selected by default, and choose from the list the blending mode **Multiply**.

To create a duplicate layer, drag it to the **Create a new layer** icon by using the **Duplicate Layer** option in the context menu of the panel or by using the **Layer** menu in the **Menu Bar**.

3. Photoshop multiplies the base color by the blend color, which results in a darker shade. However, note that the background of the image is too dark, since the blending mode is applied to the entire image; not just to one particular part. To change the background of the image into the original brightness use the layer marks. Press the **Alt** key on your keyboard and, without releasing it, click on the **Add layer mask** icon, which is the icon represented by a box with a circle inside it on the bottom of the **Layers** panel.

4. As you can see in the panel, a black layer mask has been added, which hides the layer corresponding to the blending mode **Multiply**. Now you need to manually paint those areas located in the close-up, which from the beginning you were interested in retouching. To do this, if necessary, click on the curved double arrow in the Tools panel, which is the icon used to reverse the foreground and background colors, so that the foreground color turns white.

5. Then select the **Brush Tool**, the eighth icon in the Tools panel, and adjust the master diameter to about 80 pixels in the tool Options Bar.

6. Now simply paint, the part of the image you want to darken by clicking on it while ignoring the part you do not want to darken or where the lighting is adequate. The final results will have a better balance of the flash light.

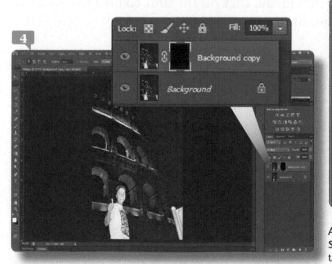

If you press the **Alt** key while creating the **layer mask**, it will be generated in black. If you do not press this key, the mask will be white.

Adjust the parameters **Size** and **Hardness** by taking into account the characteristics of the image you are working with.

Fixing digital noise

WE UNDERSTAND DIGITAL NOISE AS the values which have been read incorrectly. Because of that error, especially in areas with insufficient image lighting, a series of red, green, and blue dots appear, which cause a loss of sharpness. With Photoshop, digital noise can be reduced by changing the color mode of the image without damaging it, or by using the Reduce Noise command.

1. If you do not have your own image with digital noise, you can use file **009.jpg**. It often happens that when taking pictures with a digital camera that the color mode is RGB, so check this in the tab of the document in Photoshop. The first step you need to carry out in order to remove the digital noise in the image is directly related to the color mode. Open the **Image** menu, click on the **Mode** command and choose **Lab Color**. [1]

2. The RGB mode has three channels (Red, Green, and Blue) and the Lab Color mode consists of a luminance component and two basic colors: (a) between green and red and (b) between blue and yellow. Select channel **a**, which consists of color data and can be found in the **Channels** panel. [2]

3. Open the **Filter** menu, click on the **Blur** command and select the **Gaussian Blur** option. [3]

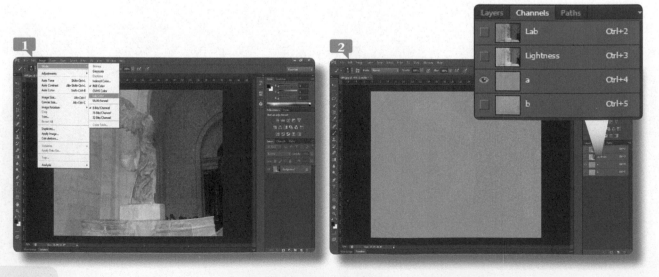

4. Enter a value in the field **Radius** in the dialog box of the filter and consider that the greater the blur is, the better the correction will be and press **OK**.

5. Select channel **b** in the **Channels** panel and repeat the steps above to apply the same filter with the same value. (You can carry out the application without opening the dialog box by pressing the keys **Ctrl + F**.)

6. When apply the blur to both color channels, you can change the image to its original color mode RGB. To do this, open the **Image** menu, click on the **Mode** command and select the **RGB Color** option.

7. Maybe the digital noise has not completely disappeared but now it has reduced, and the image's sharpness has been improved. Photoshop has a command to reduce digital noise directly. To restore the image's digital noise you can close and open the image again without saving the changes or you can click on the first action in the **History** panel.

8. Open the **Filter** menu, click on the **Noise** command and choose within the appearing submenu the **Reduce noise** option.

9. With the box **Reduce Noise** you can see the image on the left and on the right you can find the configurable parameters to solve this problem. Change them until the image has, as far as possible, reduced the existing noise. Compare the modified image with the original image in the **History** panel by applying a high zoom to see the difference.

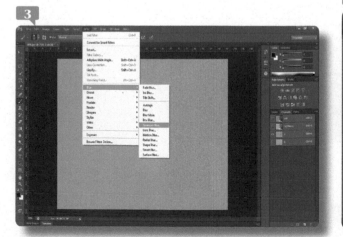

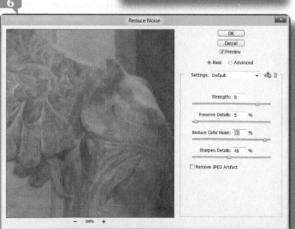

Fixing problems with underexposure

UNDEREXPOSURE IS AN ERROR directly related to the light that is captured by the sensor of a camera. In particular, dark images suffer from underexposure, which means that the exposure settings have not been sufficient enough in regard to the existing light available at the time the image was taken. Images taken against the light, or with the main light in front of the camera lens, can lead to underexposure.

1. In this lesson, we will show you a technique, which is rarely used among Photoshop users, and which helps you to correct the problem of underexposure. If you do not have a picture taken against the light, we suggest using file **010.jpg**. This image has a single background layer. To perform this technique, we need to carry out the changes on a copy of this layer. To begin, click with the right mouse button on the **Background** layer in the **Layers** panel and choose **Duplicate Layer** within the context menu.

2. Assign the term **Layer 1** for the duplicated layer in the **Duplicate Layer** dialog box and accept it. (You can also carry out the duplication by using the key combination **Ctrl + J**— in that case, the new layer appears in the panel under the default name **Layer 1**.)

3. The next step will allow you to brighten the picture with one

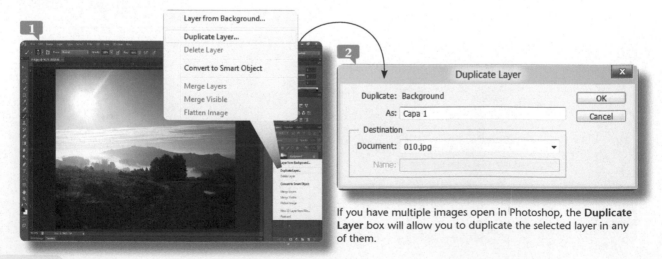

If you have multiple images open in Photoshop, the **Duplicate Layer** box will allow you to duplicate the selected layer in any of them.

010

single action. Select **Layer 1**, open the field that contains the blend modes and which display the **Normal** mode and select from the list of **Screen** options.

4. The image brightens up visually if the degree of underexposure is higher. If you need to brighten it up further, you need to duplicate the layer within the pattern as many times as necessary. We recommend using the key combination **Ctrl + J**.

5. It is possible that once you have solved the problem with underexposure in the darker parts of the image that in some part of the picture the opposite effect occurs, which is to say, an overexposure (usually in the area, in which the light enters in the front of the image). To solve this problem too, select the last duplicate layer and reduce the percentage of opacity in the relevant field of the **Layers** panel.

6. In order to finish, click on the Options button in the **Layers** panel and select the **Flatten Image** command. Thus, all duplicated layers have been grouped into the **Background** layer, keeping the new look of the image without the effect of underexposure.

You have seen that at first it seemed impossible to solve the problems of a poorly exposed photograph, but now it is very easy for users of a program like Photoshop. We encourage you to practice it with your own photographs to master these techniques.

Fixing overexposed images

IMPORTANT

You can also use the **Burn Tool**, located in the same group as the Dodge Tool, by applying it to the affected area. Like all tools, you can change its characteristics in the Options Bar.

OVEREXPOSURE OCCURS when you take a picture with too much light, which is colloquially known as "a burned photo." To avoid overexposure, it is best to make good adjustments of the f-stop or the shutter speed. However, if the digital camera you are using has a basic scale with automatic controls, these settings cannot be changed and thus, you will need to edit the image with a program like Photoshop.

1. In this exercise, you will solve a problem of overexposure in a photo with too much light. You can use your own image with this problem or sample image **011.png**. After opening the image in Photoshop, you need to use a particular blend mode that allows you to underexpose an overexposed image. The sample image illustrates the problem of overexposure only on the right-hand side of the monument, where too much light is reflected. For this reason, in this case, you only need to work on this area of the image. To start the process, display the options menu in the **Layers** panel and choose the **New Layer** command. 🗨

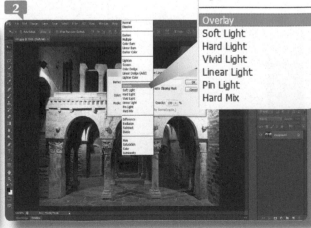

34

011

2. The difference between using this command and the corresponding icon at the bottom of the panel is that in the first case you can access the **New Layer** dialog box, while in the second, you cannot. Choose the **Overlay** option in the **Mode** field. [2]

3. Then select the check box **Fill with Overlay-neutral color (50% gray)** (note that until you choose the indicated mode, this option will be unavailable). Then click on **OK**. [3]

4. After accepting the **New Layer** in the dialog box, note the change in the **Layers** panel: a new layer filled with gray, called **Layer 1**, was created. [4] The next step is to choose an appropriate brush to paint the areas you want to underexpose— the dark areas. Click on the **Brush Tool** in the **Tools** panel. [5]

5. In the **Options Bar**, whose content has been adapted to the selected tool, choose a type of brush with a thick, soft tip, which will allow you to work comfortably. Then, in the same window, change the opacity to 30%. [6]

6. In the **Tools** panel, make sure that the selected foreground color is black and start to paint over the parts of the image you want to underexpose—the dark areas. [7]

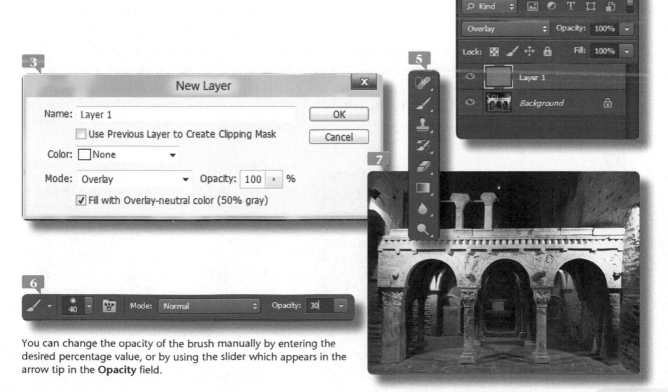

You can change the opacity of the brush manually by entering the desired percentage value, or by using the slider which appears in the arrow tip in the **Opacity** field.

Brightening up faces and objects with low light

THIS EXERCISE FOCUSES ON A SERIES OF techniques to brighten images, which are poorly exposed and are not displayed correctly. This includes, for example, shadows in the foreground that are projected on a face or an object when a snapshot is taken in natural light. In these cases, the best photographic technique prior to retouching is the use of the flash, although in many cases daylight seems to be sufficient.

1. For this exercise, you can use your own image, as long as it has a brightness problem that needs fixing, or you can use sample image **012.jpg**. There are two steps to brighten a darkened area within an image: adjust the input levels to regulate the correct exposure, which will be applied over the entire image including background, and create an exclusive brush to change only the area of interest. To carry this out, go to the **Image** menu, click on the **Adjustments** command and select the **Levels** option. **1**

2. The central graphic in the **Levels** box displays the input levels of the colors black, gray, and white, which correspond to the tones of shadows, media, and image brightness. In this case, since you want to brighten up the picture, click on the gray controller, which represents the midtones, and drag it to the left. **2**

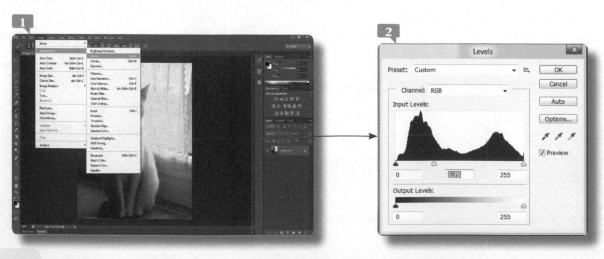

3. When you think that the element, which is located in the foreground, shows a correct exposure, click on the **OK** button.

4. To continue the process, go back to the image's original levels in order to change them with the help of the **History Brush**, but only the part of the image you are interested in. You can find it in the **History** panel in the **Window** menu. **3**

5. If you followed the steps so far, the panel should only show you two actions: **Open** and **Levels**. Then click on the first action. **4**

6. Click on the gray box that precedes the state **Levels** to fix the origin of the application of the **History Brush Tool**. **5**

7. In the **Tools** panel, select the **History Brush Tool**, which is the tenth icon from the top, **6** and choose a soft-edged and medium-sized brush from the **Options Bar**, and take into account the dimensions of the image area, which should be painted.

8. You can start to paint on the dark area of the image with the **History Brush Tool**. **7** Be aware that if the lightening effect is too intense, you may decrease it by reducing the percentage of brush opacity in the **Options Bar**.

Again, we recommend you practice this on your images until you get the best results, since the exposure used in each picture does not allow us to show in detail the values of the settings you should use to retouch them.

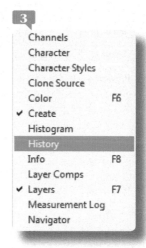

Channels
Character
Character Styles
Clone Source
Color   F6
✓ Create
Histogram
History
Info   F8
Layer Comps
✓ Layers   F7
Measurement Log
Navigator

Do not mix the **History Brush Tool** up with the **Art History Brush Tool**. With the latter you can carry out effects on the images.

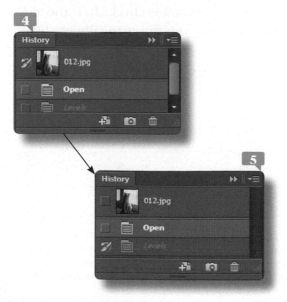

Brightening areas with deep shade

IMPORTANT

If you saved the settings specified in the Shadows/Highlights box, you can restore them by using the **Load** button in the box.

SOMETIMES YOU SHOULD USE A FLASH although the environmental conditions might make you think otherwise. A good example for this would be a beautiful image that combines the sun with shadows in a square full of trees or in a forest. In these cases, the result often shows image areas that are too shady, while the light parts have an optimal exposure. Photoshop has a command to solve this problem.

1. Outdoor images, in which the photographer has to play with sunny and shaded areas at the same time, almost always produce the same effect: dark or bright parts in contrast to others. This effect can be solved by using a full flash to brighten up the shadow areas as you take a picture, and in that way the exposure adjusts itself based on the lighter parts. With Photoshop, contrast problems with light can quickly be solved. For this exercise, you can use your own image or example file **013.jpg**. After opening the image you want to retouch, go to the **Image** menu, click on the **Adjustments** command and select the **Shadows/Highlights** option. 🔲1

2. In the dialog box **Shadows/Highlights** 🔲2 you can adjust the percentage of shadows and lights. The shadow areas are, by default, cleared by 35% (you can check the result on the image if the **Preview** option in this box is checked). If the auto adjustment does not satisfy you, you can manually modify it

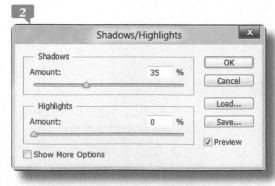

To brighten photos with good light but shadowed areas, the adjustment **Shadows/Highlights** is the most appropriate way since it lightens or darkens the image according to the adjacent pixels of the shadows or of the highlights.

013

by typing into the appropriate fields the percentage you wish, or by moving the regulators of the bar for each parameter.

3. Before accepting the dialog box and applying the new setting of the shadows definitively, get to know the other options that are related to these parameters. Enable the **Show More Options** option.

4. In the present case, which is to say the correction of the shadows, the parameter **Tonal Width** in the **Shadows** section can help you adjust the shadow areas you would like to retouch. Thus, for example, if you just want to focus on the darkest areas, you should decrease the value of that field, since if you increase it, the settings will affect a wider range of shades of the image, regardless of its intensity.

5. If you increase the shadow details too much, sometimes the colors of the image can become saturated. You can fix this in the **Adjustments** section by using the parameter **Color Correction**, where it will be necessary to reduce the saturation value.

6. As always, we recommend you practice this with your own images until you find the best settings for each case. Apply the correction by clicking on the **OK** button and have a look at the result.

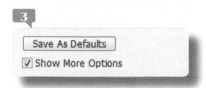

You can save the defined settings in the Shadows/Highlights box and set them as default settings for new images.

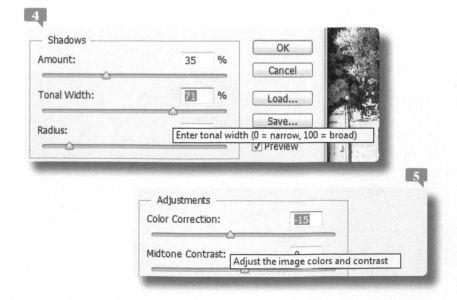

Removing red-eye effect

RED-EYE EFFECT DUE TO the flash is very common in images of people and animals and occurs because the pupil dilates when there is a lack of light. Although today most digital cameras have a control that prevents the occurrence of this effect, you can fix it later with minimal retouching in Photoshop.

1. Open the Photoshop workspace and the image in which you want to remove the red-eye effect. If you do not have your own image with this effect, you can use sample file **014.jpg**. In the **Tools** panel, click on the seventh icon and select the **Red Eye Tool**. 🔲

2. The **Options Bar** displays the parameters **Pupil Size** and **Darken Amount** with intermediate values. To correct the effect, simply click on the pupils. 🔲

3. If the color of the pupil is not the right one, change the percentage of the **Darken Amount** field. Although this technique is the quickest way to fix the red eyes, Photoshop allows you to go a little bit further by keeping the original eye color after removing the red eye effect. In the **History** panel, click on the state **Open** 🔲 to apply the original state to the image and then increase the visualization of the area of the eye by using the **Zoom** tool.

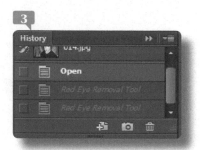

The Red Eye tool colors the pupil of the eye black. The **size of the pupil**, which can be found in the Options bar, increases or decreases the affected area by the tool.

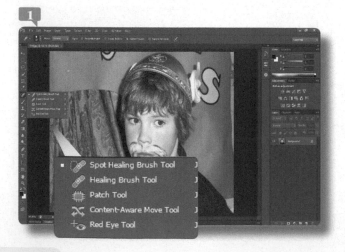

014

4. In order to continue, select the **Magic Wand Tool**, which shares space in the toolbar with the **Quick Selection Tool**, and click on the part with the red color. Then, enable the **Add to selection** option in the **Options Bar** and by playing with tolerance, click on the red area of the other eye in order to select it as well.

5. Press the key combination **Ctrl + Shift + U**.

6. Make sure that the foreground color is black, then select the **Brush Tool**, which can be found in the **Options Bar**, set the brush to a suitable diameter and a minimum hardness then adjust the opacity to **20%**.

7. Continue to click inside of each selection area until they acquire a dark gray. When finished, press the key combination **Ctrl + D** to delete the selection.

8. Then you will solve the problem of the color of the iris with the **Lasso Tool**. Select the tool, which is the third icon in the **Tools** panel, and pull to create a selection that marks the iris of one eye. Select the other eye the same way.

9. Press the key combination **Ctrl + J** while having the new layer selected, open the **Image** menu, click on the **Adjustments** command and select the **Hue/Saturation** option.

10. Select the **Colorize** option to adjust the regulators until you find the desired color and press the **OK** button to apply.

11. Use the **Eraser** tool to eliminate the parts of the image that got selected and have been colored as well. If the chosen color is too intense, you can reduce its opacity in the **Layers** panel.

12. In order to finish, open the Options menu of the **Layers** panel and select the **Flatten Image** command.

You can also add other elements to the selection by pressing **Shift** while clicking on the image.

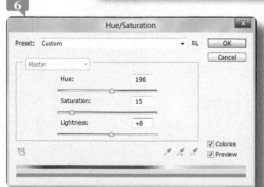

Corrosión the RGB colors

Correcting the RGB colors

IMPORTANT

It is possible to save the configuration of curves so you do not have to repeat the process on every picture you want to correct. To do this, click on the icon located on the right of **Preset** in the Curves dialog box and choose the **Save Preset** option. Then choose a location in the dialog box **Save** and click on the button **Save**.

Save Preset...
Load Preset...

Delete Current Preset

The **Curves** box is one of the most used boxes by professional photographers since it gives lots of control over the color.

ALTHOUGH ANY digital photography may seem, at a glance, correct in terms of color, it is most likely that images need to be retouched to appear more natural.. This exercise shows you how to carry out color corrections of images in the RGB mode. This is a very common action, because almost all digital cameras produce a dominant color, which is usually red or to a lesser extent blue.

1. In order to start, open the image you want to retouch in Photoshop (any RGB image, in which you can find a dominant color, either red or blue, for example the image **015.jpg**).

2. Go to the **Image** menu, click on the **Adjustments** command and select the **Curves** option. ▣

3. The color correction RGB of an image consists of three actions: the correction of the shadow areas, the areas of brightness, and the midtone areas. Double-click on the first icon of the **Eyedropper Tool**, which is called **Sample in image to black point**.

4. In the color selector you need to enter the appropriate values to set the color of the shadow areas that will serve to eliminate any dominant color in them. The fields to modify are R, G, and B. Enter the same value in all three colors (you can try a value of about **20**, but it depends on the photograph you are using) and press **OK**. ▣

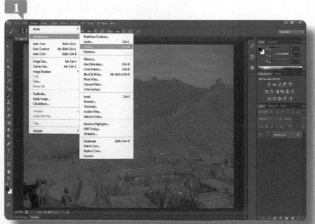

5. After solving the configuration of the shadow areas, you need to modify the areas of brightness. To do this, double-click on the third icon of the **Eyedropper Tool**, which is called **Sample in image to set white point**.

6. Enter the same value in all three fields (you can try a value of about 240, which converts the primitive white into a light gray tone, which you are interested in to neutralize the areas of brightness) and press **OK**. 3️⃣

7. You also need to close the **Curves** box by clicking on the **OK** button and click on **Yes** in the dialog box that appears.

8. Then open the menu for the **Eyedropper Tool**, which you can find in the **Tools** panel, and select the **Color Sampler Tool**. 4️⃣

9. Mark consecutively with a click the darkest and the brightest part of the image and access the **Curves** box by pressing the **Ctrl + M**. 5️⃣

10. Select the tool **Sample in image to set black point** and click on the marker **1** of the image. Then do the same (with the corresponding tool) with the brightness by clicking on the marker **2**.

11. To lighten the midtones, click on the center of the line, which divides the grid, and pull it without releasing the mouse button until you consider the correction of these tones to be accurate. Apply the correction by clicking on the **OK** button. 6️⃣

3

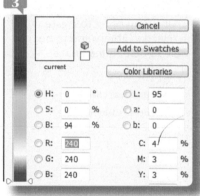

When you select the tool for the **areas of the brightness**, the values R, G, and B show the value of 255, the equivalent configuration to the white color in a palette.

4

6

5

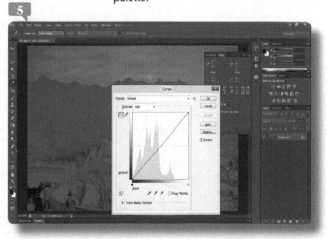

While taking the **color samples**, two markers will appear on the image, which indicate the darkest and the brightest point.

Modifying the color channels

Learning to use retouch with Photoshop CS6 and the retouch exercises

THE COLOR VALUES OF AN IMAGE change depending on its color mode. So when we convert an image from a color mode to another, their values are also modified. The Multichannel mode uses 256 levels of gray in each channel and is often used to print special images. When you convert an image in the Multichannel mode, the colors change into spot color channels of the image in which the new grayscale information is defined in terms of pixels of each color channel.

1. In this exercise you will learn to manipulate the color channels of images. To do this, you can use sample file **016.jpg**, which is an RGB image consisting of three channels: red, green, and blue. You can see which channel corresponds to which part of the image by hiding any of these channels. In the **Channels** panel, click on the visibility box in the **Red** channel.

2. When hiding the Red channel, the full image shows predominantly the color blue. Re-enable the **Red** channel.

3. To continue, click on the visibility box in the **Blue** channel to hide it.

4. Now, the predominant color is yellow. Click on the visibility box in the **Red** channel to disable it as well.

5. The image is now displayed in black and white. To restore all

You can save each of the resulting images as you hide them in the different color channels in the **Channels** panel.

016

original colors to the image, click on the visibility box in the **RGB** channel.

6. Then convert the image to the CMYK mode by using the menu path **Image/Mode/CMYK Color**.

7. In the **Channels** panel, hide the channels **Magenta** and **Yellow**.

8. Now, the only existing color in the image is blue, since it is the only one that remains active, apart from black. Let's see what happens if you hide the channel. Click on the visibility box in the **Black** channel, check if the image has lost all colors, and then click on the **Magenta** channel to display it again.

9. Click on the visibility box in the **Yellow** channel to restore the yellow color, check if the lack of black causes a loss in definition for some areas and activate the **Black** channel to display all colors again.

10. Finally, convert the CMYK image into a multichannel image. Go to the **Image** menu, click on **Mode** and select the **Multichannel** option.

11. The **Channels** panel displays four inks: cyan, magenta, yellow, and black. To hide the **Cyan** channel, click on its visibility box and then hide the **Yellow** channel.

12. Restore the yellow color by clicking on the visibility box in the Yellow channel and finish this exercise.

The color mode **CMYK** consists of four inks: cyan, magenta, yellow, and black.

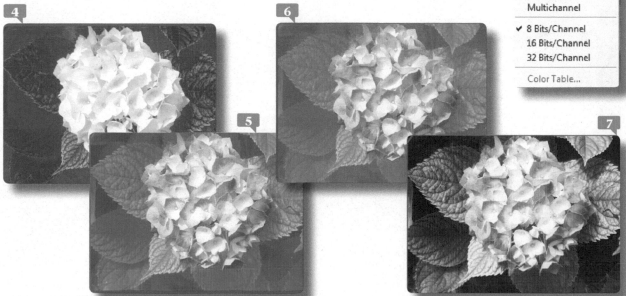

Matching the tone of two images

THE MATCH COLOR FUNCTION, which can be found in the Adjustments command of the Image menu, allows you to match the colors of multiple images, of multi-layers, or of multiple selections. The color adjustment is performed by modifying the luminance and the color chart, and by neutralizing a dye. You should be aware that this setting only works with images in the RGB mode.

1. Open both images whose color tone you want to match in Photoshop (you can also use sample files **017-001.jpg** and **017-002.jpg**).

2. In the example, the lighting of each image is different. (Enable the **Tile All Vertically** option, which can be found in the **Arrange** command in the **Window** menu to see both images). While having the image file you want to repair activated, go to the **Image** menu, click on the **Adjustments** option and select **Match Color.**

3. This opens the **Match Color** dialog box, where you first need to select the original photo that shows the tone you want to apply to the target image. Open the **Source** menu in the **Image Statistics** section and select the adequate photo.

If you do not select any part of the image, the **Match Color** option will perform a global statistic to equal them both.

017

4. When selecting the original image, the tonality is automatically applied to the target image (you can see the effect if you have enabled the **Preview** option in the dialog box). It is possible that by accident the picture is too dark or too light. To solve this problem, you can use the brightness slider. Drag it to the right to lighten the image or to the left to darken it.

5. You can also modify the saturation level of the colors by dragging the slider **Color Intensity**. Do this until you obtain the desired color.

6. Should the effect be too intense, drag the regulator **Fade** to the right.

7. Finally, to neutralize the color dyes, enable the **Neutralize** option.

8. Before applying the definite setting, you need to save this configuration to restore and apply it to other images. Click on the button **Save Statistics**.

9. Enter in the **Name** field of the **Save** box a descriptive name for the statistics of the image and, after selecting the folder where you want to save it, click on the button **Save**.

10. From now on, you can use the **Load Statistics** button to restore the settings and apply them automatically to other images. Click on the **OK** button to match the colors and check if the tones of the original image have been applied to the target image so that the colors match.

IMPORTANT

With Photoshop you can individually use the controls of the **Match Color** function to apply a single correction to the image. For example, you can adjust the **Luminance** slider to lighten or darken an image without affecting the color.

3

The image statistics are stored in the format **sta**.

5

In addition to matching the colors of two images, the **Match Color** function also allows you to match the color between different layers of the same image.

Transforming an image into black and white

A PICTURE IN BLACK AND WHITE can be more spectacular than the same image in color. Black and white pictures provide an intense sense of contrast and depth, which color images sometimes fail to achieve. The usage of the color mode Grayscale is a good solution to convert a color picture into black and white, but Photoshop offers other techniques that produce images with better resolution than the original ones.

1. To perform this exercise, use any digital image you have stored on your computer or sample image **018.jpg**. Open it in Photoshop, go to the **Image** menu, click on the **Mode** command and select the **Grayscale** option.

2. Before converting the image, the program launches a dialog box that requests the confirmation of the color removal. Click on the button **Discard** 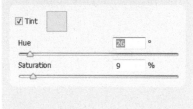 and see the result.

3. As noted above, this is not the only method to convert an image to black and white. With the tool **Black & White**, included in the **Adjustments** command of the **Image** menu or also in the **Adjustments** panel, you can create monochrome images and adjust the ink and the tonal values quickly and easily. Further, it also offers a gallery of pre-established settings that simulate filters of color, of high contrast, of neutral density, and of infrared. Restore the original image and click on the third icon in the second row in the **Adjustments**

IMPORTANT

If you convert an image to black and white by using the dialog box **Black & White** instead of the adjustment panel, it may also modify the tone and the saturation of the hue applied to the effect.

Check the change of the color information in the tab of the document as well as in the Color panel, which is produced by passing an image to a grayscale.

panel, which corresponds to the **Black & White** function.

4. The program applies some predetermined values to convert the image to black and white. Let's look at some of the pre-established settings. Click on the button of the arrowhead of the **Preset** field in the **Properties** panel and select the **Blue Filter** option.

5. See how the look of the image changes  and click on the **Auto** button to return to the monochrome predetermined setting.

6. There is still another technique. Restore the original image, open the **Image** menu, click on the **Mode** command and select **Lab Color**.

7. Enable the **Channels** panel and note that this color mode separates the brightness, which can be found in the channel **Lightness** of the color data included in the channels **a** and **b**. Since what interests us is the image in a gray or black and white scale, which is shown in the **Lightness** channel, select it and have a look at the change.

8. Open the **Image** menu, click on the **Mode** command and select the **Grayscale** mode again, in order to confirm the elimination of the other channels.

9. The existing channels have disappeared and been replaced by one which is called **Gray**. Go to the **Layers** panel and duplicate the **Background** layer by pressing **Ctrl + J**.

10. With the new layer enabled, select the **Multiply** blending mode.

11. When applying this blending mode to the new layer, the image is normally too dark, which is why it is necessary to adjust the tone manually. To do this, decrease the percentage of **opacity** until you like it and finish the exercise.

018

The **Adjustments** panel includes the necessary tools to establish adjustments and to create masks and fillings.

In Photoshop CS6, the properties of the Black & White adjustment are carried out from the **Properties** panel, where you can choose between different types of pre-established filters.

Editing a grayscale image with the Channel Mixer

IN ADDITION TO THE TECHNIQUES in the previous exercise, it is also possible to convert a color image into black and white by using the Channel Mixer. This technique is preferred by many professionals because it allows you to merge the three RGB channels to get an image with a personalized grayscale.

1. Open the image, which you want to convert into grayscale, in Photoshop and click on the **Channel Mixer** icon, the fifth icon in the second row in the **Adjustment** panel.

2. You can also access the Channel mixer from the submenu **Adjustments** in the **Image** menu, but if you use the **Adjustment** panel, the mixer is added as an adjustment layer in the **Layers** panel and thus, allows you to restore the original image at any time.  To convert your grayscale image, click on the check box in the **Monochrome** option in the **Properties** panel of the setting.

3. Thus, the RGB channels merge into a grayscale.  Now you can use the regulators Red, Green, and Blue to match the per-

The Channel Mixer is, by default, configured to merge the color in the RGB channels.

The **Monochrome** option sets the gray as an output channel and creates a color image that just contains gray values.

019

centages of each channel and to create the desired grayscale effect. Change these percentages until you obtain the desired result. 5

4. Go to the Properties panel and also drag the slider **Constant** to adjust the overall brightness of your image in grayscale. 6

5. The slider **Constant** is used to adjust the grayscale value of the selected output channel. Negative values add more black and positive values add more white. You can also use some of the pre-established settings of the Channel Mixer to produce stunning effects. Open the Channel Mixer menu, which now displays the **Custom** option and select, for example, the setting **Black & White with Orange Filter (RGB)**. 7

6. Notice how the percentages change in the fields Red, Green, Blue, and Constant as you apply this setting. To eliminate the adjustment layer **Channel Mixer** you can use the trash can icon, which appears at the bottom of the **Properties** panel, or you can drag the layer to the trash can icon in the **Layers** panel. Delete this layer now by clicking the trash can icon. 8

7. Confirm that you want to delete the adjustment layer by clicking on the **Yes** button in the warning box that appears. 9

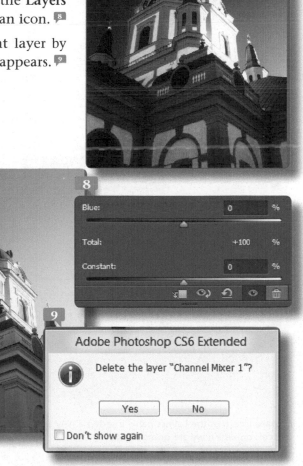

Photoshop displays the total percentage of the original channels in the **Total** field of the mixer. If this percentage exceeds 100%, a warning icon will appear.

Converting to extreme grayscale

BY ADJUSTING THE REGULATORS of the Channel Mixer properly, it is possible to obtain spectacular effects. For example, if you have a picture of a mountain landscape and you want to add an intense contrast and perspective with the mixer, you will get an inversion in an extreme grayscale.

1. For this exercise, use one of your pictures or sample file **020. jpg**. In the same way as in the previous lesson, open the **Channel Mixer** by clicking on the fifth icon in the second row of the **Adjustment** panel.

2. To change the output channel into gray and to convert the photo into black and white, enable the **Monochrome** option in the **Properties** panel of the adjustment. **1**

3. In this exercise, we will give you approximate values, which will lead to the extreme effect that you are searching for, but, as always, you need to change the sliders to obtain the desired result in each case. Double-click on the percentage field of the **Red** channel and enter the value **160**. **2**

4. Continue by dragging the slider of the **Green** channel to the

Make sure that the **Layers** panel inserted a new adjustment layer, on which we are going to work.

Remember that you can use the mixer in the submenu Adjustments of the Image menu, although you will lose the color information of the original image.

right until it reaches **190** percent. (Of course, you can also write that value in the numeric field.) 3

5. These two changes in the percentages of the channels have caused too much light in the image, so the next step will be to restore the details and to create extreme shadows. To do this, double-click on the percentage field of the **Blue** channel and enter the value -200. 4

6. The process could not be easier and faster and the result is spectacular. Depending on the photo you are working with, you may need to increase or decrease the values of the channel or if you need to modify the **Constant** slider in order to add or eliminate brightness. In this example, double-click on the **Constant** field, enter the value **-15** 5 and check the result on the image. 6

7. To compare the appearance of the original image with the modified one, hide the adjustment layer temporarily by clicking on the eye icon on the left of the layer in the **Layers** panel and show it again by clicking on the same icon.

As you can see, what in the beginning may seem a bit complicated, only requires a few steps due to the adjustment functions of the Channel Mixer. Feel free to investigate on your own by using your own pictures in order to get to know the potential of this tool.

Creating duotones

A DUOTONE IS THE USE OF TWO INKS applied to a grayscale image. It is recommended in cases when you are printing a photograph in spot colors. To convert an image to a duotone, it has to be in the Grayscale mode. In the process of conversion to a duotone, you must specify the amount of each ink, and you need to edit the duotone curves to determine the overlap of inks.

1. If you do not have any grayscale images, open a photograph in Photoshop and convert it to grayscale following the path **Image/Mode/Grayscale** and confirm that you want to discard the color information.

2. Open the **Image** menu again, click on the **Mode** command and select the **Duotone** option. 🔲

3. As you open the **Duotone Options** box for the first time, you will see that the **Monotone** option is selected. This option is only selected when you want to use one ink to print a picture in black. Open the **Type** field and select the **Duotone** option. 🔲

4. Then choose the two inks you want to use for the printing. The first ink, which is set by default, is black. The box **Duotone Curve**, which displays a diagonal line next to the field **Ink 1**, allows you to determine the color distribution you want to select for the highlights, the midtones, and the shad-

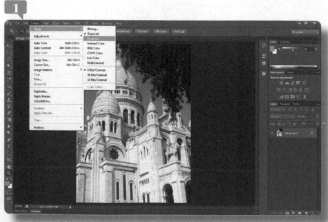

When you use two inks, as in the case of a duotone, they overlap, and this results in the printing of the basic color combinations.

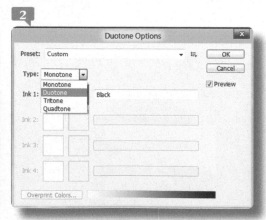

As you can see, in the **Type** field you can also select the options **Tritone** and **Quadtone**, and hence, a third or fourth ink.

ows. Keep the black ink as Ink 1 and click on the white box for the second ink.

5. In the **Color Picker (Ink 2 Color)** box you can choose the color you like most, in order to configure the duotone mode of your image. Select a color and click on the **OK** button.

6. You can type the name of the chosen color in the field **Ink 2**. As you can see, the result is immediately shown on the image and you can choose to end the process here. However, to continue, we will show you how to configure the duotone curve, where you will be able to adjust the balance between the two inks. Click on the box that displays a diagonal line corresponding to Ink 2.

7. The **Duotone Curve** box opens automatically for that ink. The fact that the graphic grid line is straight indicates that the image takes the same amount of both inks in all areas (highlights, midtones, and shadows). The adjustment of the intermediate values displays more or less light or shadows on the image, always in respect to the ink with which you are working. The adjustment of the duotone curve can be performed directly on the chart—a perhaps more direct way if it does not dominate the field values.

8. When you have finished adjusting the duotone curve, click on the **OK** button to get back to the **Duotone Options** dialog box, in which you can check if the shown duotone curve has adapted the shape, which was configured in the previous box. Also click on **OK** to apply the image changes and have a look at the effect that you have achieved.

In the **Duotone Curve** box, the maximum value of shadow corresponds to the field 100, the value of the midtones is 50, and the first value of illumination is 0.

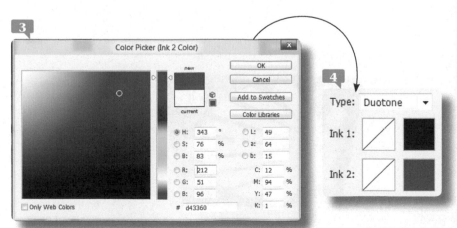

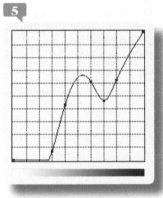

Selecting with precision

SELECTING PRECISELY is directly linked to any act of retouching or editing in parts of an image. That is why it is essential to get to know the appropriate tools to carry out this action. This exercise will demonstrate how to use the Pen Tool, whose main characteristic is the ability to draw straight lines or curves of any shape and which also allows the selection of any shape.

1. In the first part of this exercise, you will use the **Pen Tool** to select a shape with a straight contour, and in the second part you will select curved shapes. You can use any photo or if you prefer, you can use sample file **022.jpg**. Open the image in Photoshop and enable the **Pen Tool** in the **Tools** panel (the icon that looks like a fountain pen nib).

2. Before starting to select the image area that interests you, make sure that the **Path** option in the Options Bar is enabled. 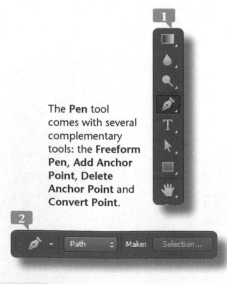 The paths become apparent by clicking on the vertices of the figure, which you want to select. Click on one of the vertices of the blue box in the image to fix the first point of the selection.

3. Click on a second vertex of the box to fix the second point. The result of this action should be a straight line between two points.

IMPORTANT

Photoshop offers the **Refine Edge** command in the **Select** menu, with which it is possible to improve the quality of the edges of the selection. You can see the selection with different backgrounds to facilitate its edition. This option is the ideal complement to any of the selection tools that the program provides.

The **Pen** tool comes with several complementary tools: the **Freeform Pen, Add Anchor Point, Delete Anchor Point** and **Convert Point**.

To work more accurately, **expand the visualization zoom** of the image. You can do this without changing the tool by clicking on the Alt key and moving the mouse.

022

4. Continue to trace the selection around the figure in the same way, that is by clicking on each of its vertices.

5. The selection must be completed by clicking on the starting point again. Now the figure is fully surrounded by this path. Press the key combination **Ctrl + Enter** to convert the path into a selection. 🔲

6. After selecting the figure, you can start to manipulate the image. The **Pen Tool** does not only allow the selection of straight contours, but of curved forms as well. We should note that the first time you try to create curved drawings, it may seem a little complicated, since the technique requires some skills, which will undoubtedly come with practice. So do not give up! Begin the path by marking the starting point with the **Pen Tool**.

7. Move your mouse by clicking and holding the mouse button, then drag it to create the curved path by the contour of the shape. You choose the curvature of the path, so when you think the profile fits perfectly, click again. 🔲 Repeat the steps until you close the form by clicking on the first point.

8. Press the key combination **Ctrl + Enter** to convert the path to a selection. 🔲

A selection segment can be removed if the line does not fit the profile properly by clicking on the **Delete** key. Thus, only the last segment is deleted, and if you want to delete the entire selection up to this point, press the **Backspace** key.

Before converting the path to a selection, you can modify the inserted points with the **Path Selection Tool**, whose icon is a white arrow and which can be found in the Tools panel. With it, you can click on the item you want to change, drag it and reposition it.

Repairing or removing skin flaws

RETOUCHING IMAGES OF PEOPLE is one of the techniques that professionals turn to most in photography. In magazines, newspapers, or advertisements it is common to see faces and bodies with perfect skin, although the reality is very different. This exercise shows you some techniques that are used in Photoshop to repair imperfections of facial skin.

1. In this exercise you can use example image **023.jpg**. You will repair the subject's skin by copying the texture of the skin over the area you want to repair. Begin by zooming in on the face. Click on the **Clone Stamp Tool**, the ninth icon in the **Tools** panel.

2. In the **Options Bar**, open the **Brush Picker** and choose one with a soft tip (with 0% hardness) and a size slightly larger than the flaw you want to repair.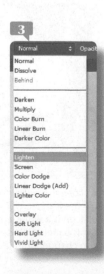

3. Then select a blending mode by which the repairing only affects the pixels darker than the chosen area displays. In the same bar, open the **Mode** list, which displays the **Normal** mode, and select the **Lighten** option.

4. The next step is to chose a skin area that has no imperfection and then stick it on the affected part. When you have located the right part, press the **Alt** key and, without releasing it, click on it.

The **Clone Stamp Tool** can also be found in the Tools panel under **Pattern Stamp**.

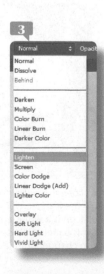

In Photoshop CS6, **new brushes** have been added to the gallery.

5. It is important to choose an example as close as possible to the area that you want to repair, and in this way, while carrying out the bonding, the pixels will coincide with the part that is not perfect. Click on this imperfection. 4

6. This is the quickest and easiest technique to remove skin flaws. Another technique involves the use of the **Lasso** selection tool. (Practice it with the same image by restoring its original state, or open a new one.) Select this tool in the **Tools** panel and draw a selection area as close as possible to the imperfection. 5

7. Open the **Select** menu, click on the **Modify** command and select the **Feather** option.

8. In the **Feather Selection** box, enter a very small value, such as **2 pixels** and click **OK**. 6

9. To copy and paste the selected area on the object that needs to be retouched, click at the same time on the **Ctrl** and **Alt** key and drag the selection to the area that needs to be repaired. 7

10. Press the key combination **Ctrl + D** to eliminate the selection and to check the result of the retouch.

11. You can also repair facial flaws with the **Healing Brush Tool**. After changing the image to its original state, select that tool, 8 which is the seventh icon in the Tools Palette and in the **Options Bar** select a brush size with a broad end, which is slightly larger than the flaw.

12. To obtain a skin sample that will be used for the repairing, press the **Alt** key and click on the chosen area. Apply the chosen area as an example by clicking on the area you want to repair and check the result.

IMPORTANT

By clicking on the **Alt** key to get the sample with the Clone Stamp or Healing Brush Tool, the mouse pointer displays a crosshair.

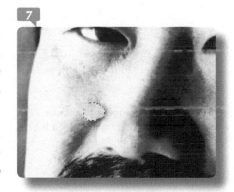

Unifying the skin tone in RGB

ALTHOUGH BRIGHTNESS, MIDTONES, AND SHADOWS are adjusted correctly in the Curves box, the skin tones of your image may still be too red. To solve this problem and to get a proper skin tone by removing the excess red color, follow these steps.

1. In Photoshop, open an image you want to retouch (if you want you can use the sample file, **024.jpg**).

2. Select the skin areas, which are too red, with the **Lasso Tool**. Enable it in the Tools panel and by using the drag technique, select the adequate areas. (You can add other selection areas if the **Add to Selection** option is enabled in the **Options Bar** or by pressing the **Shift** key and continue with the selection of other areas.)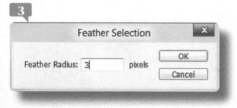

3. To smooth the edges of the selection so that the edges do not look too sharp in the target areas, you should blur them. Go to the **Select** menu, click on **Modify** and select the **Feather** option.

4. In the **Feather Selection** box, enter in the field **Feather Radius** the value 3 (this value should be adjusted according to the image you are working with) and press **OK**.

5. Then go to the **Image** menu, click on the **Adjustments** com-

You can also blur the edges of a selection with the Lasso by specifying a value in the **Feather** field of the Options Bar.

You can also access the Feather Selection box by pressing the key combination **Shift + F6**.

mand and select the **Hue/Saturation** option.

6. Press the arrow tip of the field that displays the value **Master** and select the **Reds** option to adjust this tone for the selected areas.

7. Enable the **Preview** option in this box to see the effect of adjustment on the image before applying it permanently. The last step is to reduce the saturation so that the skin tones look more natural. Drag the **Saturation** slider to the left to reduce the amount of the red. When the preview shows you the desired result, apply the setting by clicking on the **OK** button.

8. Press the key combination **Ctrl + D** to deselect the skin areas.

9. To compare the appearance of the original image with the modified one, access the **History** panel and have a look at the state **Open** and then on the last state, which should be **Deselect**. The change is noticeable: now, the skin tones are much more natural.

Again, we recommend you practice on your own with your own photographs to see how a simple retouch can make remarkable improvements.

024

IMPORTANT

For portraits, which should be printed with a printing press instead of a color printer (catalogs, brochures, etc.) the technique to correct skin tones is to **balance the magenta and yellow** in those tones, so that in the photograph there is between 3 and 5% more yellow than magenta. You can achieve this in the Curves box, by checking the values in the Information panel.

If your entire image is too red, you can make this adjustment in the saturation of reds without having anything selected

61

Removing rings under the eyes

TO ELIMINATE UNAESTHETIC RINGS UNDER THE EYES in a portrait, you can use the Clone Stamp Tool or Patch Tool. In the previous exercise, you learned how to use the Clone Stamp Tool by taking a sample of clean skin and good texture from the face and applying it to the area that needed to be corrected. The Patch tool, however, is used to select the affected area and drag it to the area that needs to be corrected.

1. To begin, open the image you want to retouch in Photoshop (you can also use example image **025.jpg**).

2. Select the **Clone Stamp Tool** in the **Tools** panel and select a soft brush in the Brush selector of the Options Bar, which is appropriate in size to the area that needs to be corrected.

3. In the **Options Bar**, enter the value **50%** in the **Opacity** field and choose the mode **Lighten** so that the change only affects the darker areas.

4. To select an example, hold down the **Alt** key, and click as close as possible to a part of the eye that is not affected by the dark circles.

5. Then paint with the brush over the dark circles to reduce

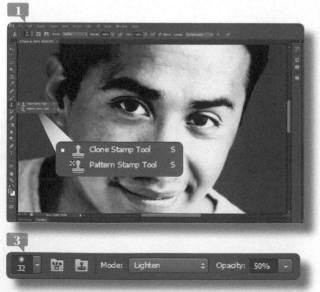

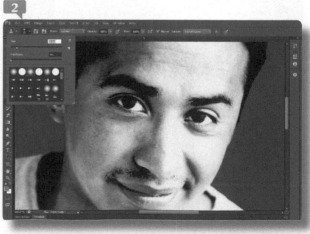

If you carried out the previous lesson with the Clone Stamp Tool, the mode **Lighten** will already be selected in the Options Bar.

or eliminate them altogether. You may have to click several times to get a perfect result. 🔲

6. Let's see how to remove rings under the eyes with the **Patch Tool**. Restore the initial appearance of the image in the **History** panel 🔲 and enable the tool, which shares space in the palette with the **Spot Healing Brush, Healing Brush, Remix,** and **Red Eye Tools.** 🔲

7. Make sure that the **Source** option in the **Options Bar** is selected and draw by dragging the selected area on the dark circles. (Remember that if you select the **Add to selection** option in the Options Bar, new selections can be created and added to the current one.) 🔲

8. After making your selection, click on it and drag it to an area of the face that does not have any blemishes. (While dragging, you can see the effect of the correction, which makes the work much easier). As you release the mouse button, the patch copies the clean area and realizes the adequate retouch.

9. To deselect the area of the dark circles and to check if the correction has been performed as expected, press the key combination **Ctrl + D.** 🔲

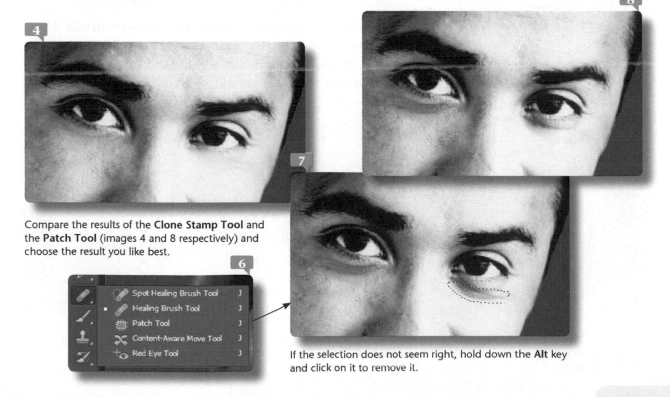

Compare the results of the **Clone Stamp Tool** and the **Patch Tool** (images 4 and 8 respectively) and choose the result you like best.

If the selection does not seem right, hold down the **Alt** key and click on it to remove it.

Eliminating freckles, acne, and other blemishes

THE TECHNIQUE SHOWN BELOW is the most used method by portrait photographers to help them reduce or eliminate large areas of acne, freckles, pockmarks, age spots, etc. Large areas can quickly and easily be fixed when you do not have time to cover imperfections.

1. Open the image you would like to work on in Photoshop. (You can also use sample file **026.jpg**.)

2. Then open the **Filter** menu, click on the **Blur** option and select the **Gaussian Blur** option. 🔲

3. In the **Gaussian Blur** box, drag the slider all the way to the left and then drag it slowly clockwise until the freckles, acne marks, etc., get out of focus and you cannot distinguish them from the rest of the complexion. Click on the **OK** button to apply the filter. 🔲

4. Now restore the initial state of the image in the **History** panel. Show the panel by selecting it from the **Window** menu. 🔲

5. This panel is complemented by the **History Brush Tool**, which allows you to paint again to get the original look of the picture, and which appears as you use the **Undo Tool**. In this case, the history states should be two: **Open** and **Gaussian**

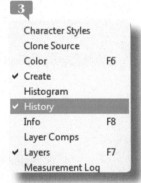

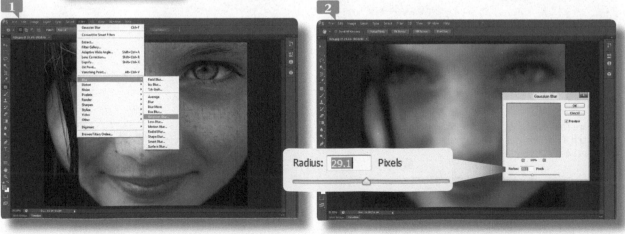

Photoshop CS6 has added **new advanced blur filters** with which you can practice further and with which you can achieve spectacular effects.

The **Gaussian Blur** filter is used to blur a selection by adjusting the quantity. Note that it produces a foggy effect.

Blur. To view the image in its original condition, click on the state **Open**.

6. Now, in the **History** panel, click on the box on the left of the **Gaussian Blur** state in order to apply in this area the original state for the History Brush Tool.

7. Now activate the **History Brush Tool**, which is the tenth icon in the **Tools** panel.

8. So that a blurred version of the photo is not painted, change the blending mode of the brush in the **Options Bar** to **Lighten**.

9. Choose an appropriate brush and paint over all the areas with acne marks, freckles, etc., until you get the perfect retouch.

Compare the original image with the retouched one by alternating between the two states of history in the **History** panel. While you paint with the **History Brush Tool**, only the pixels darker than the out of focus ones are affected. In the event that the correction leads to a too perfect appearance of the person and you would like to undo this action, try to reduce the percentage of opacity of the brush by 50%. In any case, depending on the photo you are practicing with, you should adjust the brush to achieve the desired effect.

The actions listed in the History panel are called **History States**.

With the help of the **History Brush Tool**, you can make a copy of the state indicated in the History panel to modify the image you are working on.

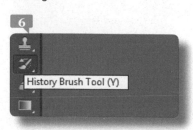

History Brush Tool (Y)

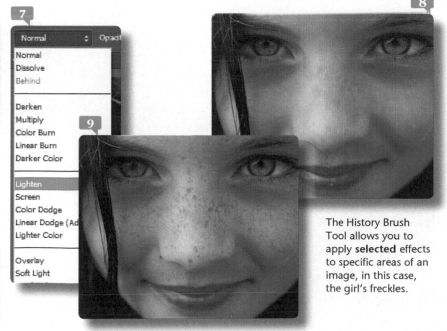

The History Brush Tool allows you to apply **selected** effects to specific areas of an image, in this case, the girl's freckles.

Removing wrinkles and other signs of aging

IMPORTANT

You can also mitigate the effect of the Healing Brush Tool by using the **Fade** option in the Edit menu. This option opens a dialog box that allows you to set the percentage of opacity of the effect.

Opacity: 100 %

THE HEALING BRUSH AND PATCH TOOLS, which were already used in previous lessons to eliminate rings under the eyes, can also be used to eliminate signs of aging such as wrinkles around the eyes and in the corners of the mouth. In this exercise you will see how to remove these signs in a professional and realistic way, but remember that wrinkles are beautiful!

1. Open the image you would like to modify in Photoshop (you can also use sample file **027.jpg**).

2. The problem we encountered when using the **Healing Brush** and **Patch Tools** while removing wrinkles and other signs of aging is that it eliminates everything, which can produce an exaggerated, rejuvenating effect. To avoid this, you need to make the corrections on a duplicate of the Background layer. Press the key combination **Ctrl + J.**

3. Select the **Healing Brush Tool** in the **Tools** panel.

4. Remember the way to get a sample for the subsequent repair is by pressing the **Alt** key and clicking on an area of the skin without blemishes.

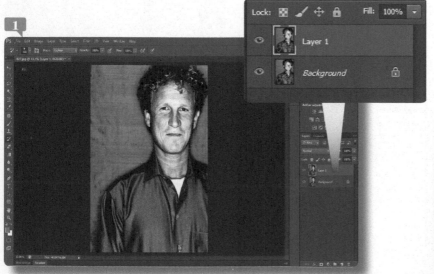

Another way to duplicate the layer is to access the **Duplicate Layer** dialog box in the Options menu of the panel, and in which you can name the layer.

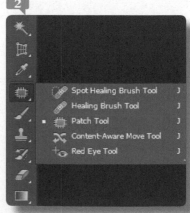

027

5. Once you have the sample, paint on the wrinkles or other signs of aging that you want to correct (around the eyes and on the forehead within the example image with which you are working with).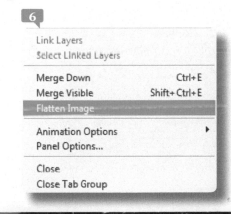

6. Note that if you click on the image for the first time, the tones may not be adequate. Do not worry because Photoshop will make quick calculations and mix the tones to even them out. Remember that you can get similar results if you use the **Patch Tool**, which allows a quick selection of a large area of the face (see the exercise "Removing rings under the eyes"). However, the total elimination of wrinkles makes it obvious that the picture has been retouched. This problem can be quickly solved. Reduce the opacity of the duplicate layer by using the **Opacity** slider in the **Layers** panel.

7. In this way, the original photo appears dim and thus, retains some of the original wrinkles, which makes the image look more realistic. Use the **Flatten image** option in the Options menu of the **Layers** panel to merge the two layers and to finish the exercise by saving a copy of the retouched image.

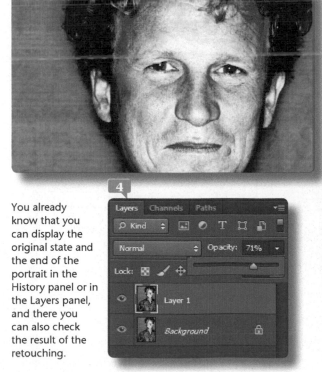

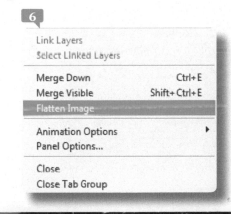

You already know that you can display the original state and the end of the portrait in the History panel or in the Layers panel, and there you can also check the result of the retouching.

Applying a blur effect to the skin

YOU HAVE SEEN ADVERTISEMENTS, magazines, and other printed materials that show pictures of people with a slightly blurred look, which considerably softens the shapes. There is a very simple technique, based on the Gaussian blur, which allows you to give faces this blurred, softened and silky look.

1. Use any picture you have stored on your computer or sample file **028.jpg**. After opening the image in Photoshop, press **Ctrl + J** to duplicate the background layer.

2. Then, go to the box that corresponds to the **Gaussian Blur** filter in order to create the blur effect on the picture. Open the **Filter** menu, click on the **Blur** option and select the said filter. ①

3. In the **Gaussian Blur** box, drag the slider to between 3 and 6 pixels (depending on the amount of blur you want to apply to the skin) and press the **OK** button. ②

4. To give the image a soft glow, reduce the opacity to **50%** of Layer 1 by entering the value in the **Opacity** field of the **Layers** panel. ③

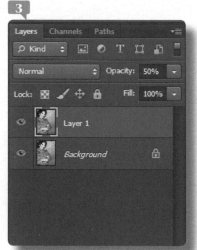

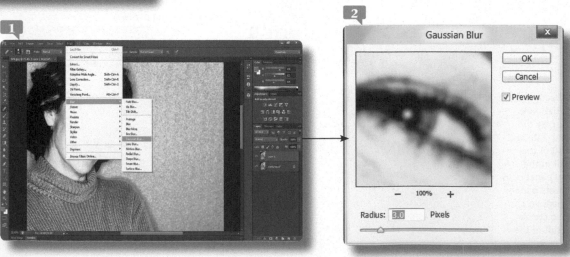

68

028

5. If the result seems correct, you can leave the image as it is. However, it may be that the face appears too blurred. This can be solved easily by using the **Eraser Tool**. Select the tool, which is the eleventh icon in the **Tools** panel.

6. In the **Options Bar**, open the Brush selector and select a soft brush.

7. Now you need to delete the parts of the face you want to highlight (such as eyes, mouth, eyebrows, teeth, etc.). In this way, the original image properties are displayed in those areas of the Background layer, which are located below Layer 1.

8. You can also try to delete only some parts of the face or you can eliminate the blur effect of the whole image except for the skin. It is up to you. If you want to delete everything except for the skin, use a coarse brush to save time and effort.

9. After achieving the desired effect, compare the original image with the retouched one by accessing the **History** panel and show and hide both states.

Select the **size** and **hardness** of the brush according to the quantity of the image you want to delete with the Eraser Tool.

You can also directly enable the **Eraser** Tool on the keyboard by pressing the **E** key. Choose the right brush tool in relation to the quantity of the image you want to delete.

Stylizing a portrait

THERE ARE DIFFERENT TECHNIQUES to make a person in an image look slimmer. The easiest one is to use the function Free Transform to reduce the width of the image. Thus, the entire subject seems slim. But it is also possible to reduce fat pads with the Liquify filter, which now in Photoshop CS6 can be applied more quickly and you can remove bellies and thighs or reduce arm sag with the Clone Stamp Tool.

1. Open the image you want to modify in Photoshop (you can use example image **029.jpg**), go to the **Select** menu and click on the **All** option. 🔲

2. After selecting the entire image, go to the **Edit** menu and click on the **Free Transform** option. 🔲

3. As you enable this function, some drawing tools will appear around the image, which will allow you to widen or narrow it, shorten or lengthen it, tip it, etc. Click on the left center drawing tool and, without releasing the mouse button, drag it to the right and see how the person in the photo appears slimmer. 🔲

You can also select the entire image by pressing the key combination **Ctrl + A**.

You can also reduce the width of the image by entering a value in the **Width** field in the **Options Bar** of the Free Transform Tool.

4. It is not recommended to narrow the image more than 95% since the effect would be too obvious. As you get the desired effect, press the **Enter** key or the **Commit transform** icon in the **Options Bar** to apply the change permanently. [4]

5. You can check the reduced width of the image at the bottom of the canvas. Click on the **Crop Tool**, [5] select the entire image except for the bottom piece and double-click on the selection to eliminate the white.

6. Now you can see how to use the improved **Liquify** filter to reduce fat pads, double chins, flabbiness, etc. In our example, try to reduce the double chin of the model. Open the **Filter** menu and select **Liquify**.

7. In the **Liquify** box, expand with the **Zoom** tool the area you want to retouch. [6]

8. Then select the tool **Push Left**, which is the fifth icon in the **Tools** panel [7] and, after selecting in the **Tool Options** section a brush size appropriate to the area you want to fix, [8] click on the double chin and outside of it until it is eliminated or at least reduced.

9. When you are finished with retouching the image, click on the **OK** button to apply the filter and have a look at the final result. [9]

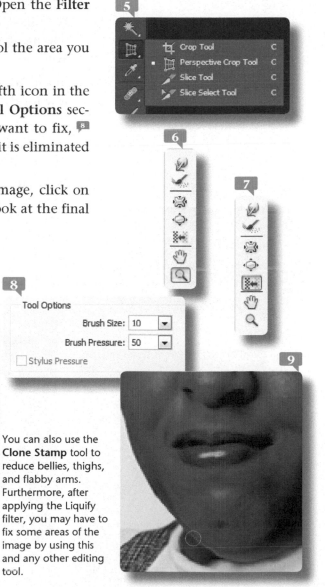

It is also possible to cancel the modifications by clicking on the no symbol, the icon of a circle with a line through it, which is located on the left of the approval icon.

You can also use the **Clone Stamp** tool to reduce bellies, thighs, and flabby arms. Furthermore, after applying the Liquify filter, you may have to fix some areas of the image by using this and any other editing tool.

Changing hair color

SEVERAL METHODS EXIST TO CHANGE the original hair color of a person in a photo. One of them is directly related to color management, which is to combine the color balance with the application of a brush over the area to be modified. The technique of adjusting the color balance of an image requires the use of mask layers, which prevent any damage to the image pixels.

1. For this exercise, you can use your own image or sample file **030.jpg**. Open the the image in Photoshop to retouch the image.

2. In the **Adjustments** panel, click the second icon in the second row for the **Color Balance** adjustment.

3. It creates a layer mask that you can see in the **Layers** panel.  The challenge now is to adjust the colors in the properties panel adjustment, depending on the tone you want to give the hair, by moving the sliders. For example, suppose you want to give a red tint to the hair, in which case, move the **Red** slider all the way to the right, until the value displayed in the color field level is +100, and then play with the other sliders to achieve the desired hair color.

4. The **Tone** section of this panel is where you can select the ar-

The balance adjustment layer affects the entire picture. Note that now the hair is shown with red tones.

030

eas to apply this percentage of color, shadows, and highlights (whichever option is selected by default, which here is **Mid-tones**). When you finish performing this adjustment, see the result on the image.

5. The layer mask covers the entire picture with a dominant color: red. Do not worry, because later you will hide this layer and paint only the hair with the color chosen. First, in the **Tools** panel, select black as the foreground color.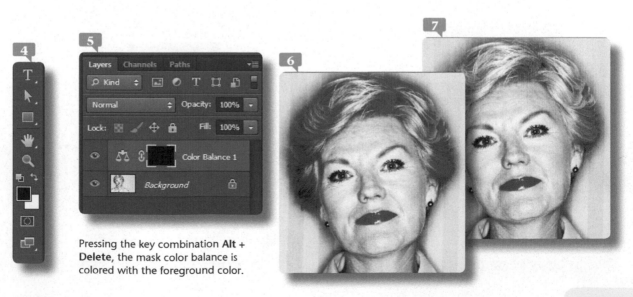

6. Now fill the **Color Balance** layer mask and at the same time remove the red color of the image. Press the key combination **Alt + Delete**.

7. The next step is to paint only the woman's hair, taking advantage of the reddish hue in the **Color Balance** layer mask. Select the **Brush Tool** in the **Tools** panel and this time choose white as the foreground color.

8. Depending on the area of hair color you need, select the **Options** to select the appropriate brush size. After setting the tool, start to paint, dragging the pointer over the hair, being careful not to go outside the boundaries. You can switch brush tips as needed.

9. Note that the application of the brush on each area will determine the tone of color. If you perform this action with precision, the result is amazing. To compare the original image with the modified image, show and hide the **Color Balance** layer in the **Layers** panel.

IMPORTANT

You can also use the **Color Balance** adjustment from the **Image** menu to change the hair color. The difference between this and the corresponding **Adjustments** panel, is that the former does not create an adjustment layer on which to make the changes. The problem with this is that you can risk damaging the original image.

Pressing the key combination **Alt + Delete**, the mask color balance is colored with the foreground color.

Whitening the eyes

BE IT DUE TO AGE OR ANY OTHER physical problem, the whites of the eyes do not always appear perfect, and the whites of the eyes can contain red or yellow spots, which are not aesthetically pleasing in a portrait. Photoshop has tools to correct these imperfections in a very simple way.

1. In this exercise you will discover one of the techniques that is used to whiten and brighten the whites of people's eyes in your photographs. You need a picture displaying this problem. If you have one, open it in the workspace. If you do not have one, you can use sample file **031.jpg**. If necessary, apply the zoom to increase the visibility of the part you want to retouch.

2. The technique that you want to carry out involves the use of the **Lasso Tool**. Select this tool in the **Tools** panel  and draw, by dragging, a path around the white of the eye. (You know that you can add selections by holding down the **Shift** key if the **Add to selection** option in the **Options Bar** is activated.)

3. In order to avoid the perception of the retouching in this area, you need to soften the edges of the selection. Go to the **Select** menu, click on the **Modify** command and select the **Feather** option.

IMPORTANT

You can also improve the appearance of the eyes by adding a layer of the Curves adjustment in the blending mode Screen, which will clarify whole picture. Then select black as the foreground color and fill the layer mask with it by pressing the combination Alt + Delete. Then choose white as the foreground color and paint with the adequate brush over the areas of the eye you want to whiten.

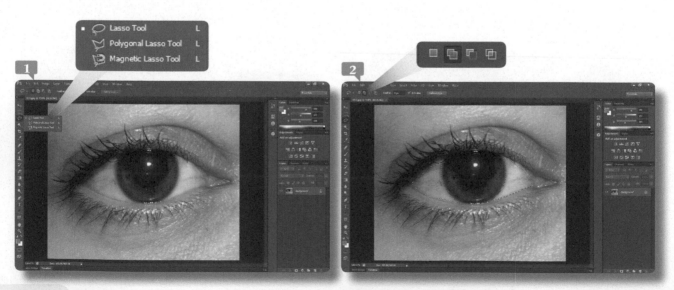

031

4. In the **Feather Selection** box, insert **2 pixels** and click on OK. [3]

5. Open the **Image** menu, click on the **Adjustments** command and select the **Hue / Saturation** option. [4]

6. Maintain the **Master** option in the channel selector of the **Hue / Saturation** box. [5]

7. The next step is to increase the brightness of the channels. To do this, drag the **Lightness** parameter to the right to increase its value and, simultaneously, the brightness of the whites of the eyes. If the **Preview** option is enabled, you can see the changes immediately in the picture. [6]

8. Note that an excessive increase of the brightness can produce an exaggerated and unnatural effect. Press the **OK** button.

9. Go back to the picture, press the key combination **Ctrl + D** to deselect the eyes, review the obtained result and compare the original [7] with the final image [8] by putting them in both states in the **History** panel.

[4]

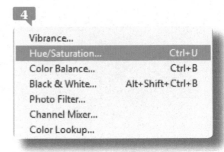

Depending on the type of retouching you are carrying out, you will need to select specific **channels** or all the channels in the Hue/Saturation box.

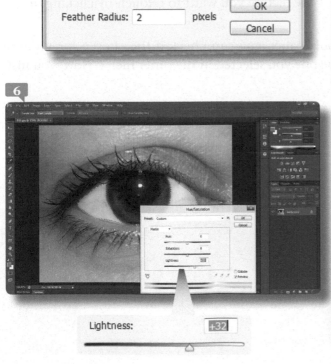

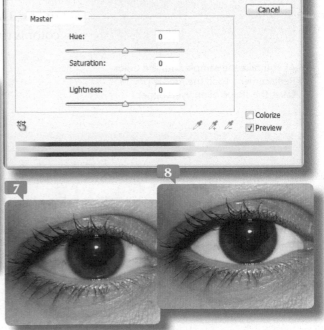

Changing eye color

IMPORTANT

You can also easily change eye color by selecting the iris and varying the **Hue/Saturation** values.

BESIDES BLEACHING, BRIGHTENING, and generally improving the appearance of the eyes, Photoshop can also quickly change the color using the Color Replacement Tool. This exercise will show you how.

1. To carry out this exercise, you can use sample images **032a. jpg** and **032b.jpg**, which, as always, you can download from our website. You will apply the eye color of the first image to the second one. To begin, open both images in Photoshop and put in the foreground the second one, the one that displays the eye color you want to apply to your photo.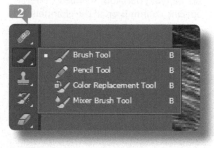

2. The **Color Replacement** Tool can be found in the **Tools** panel within the **Brush**, **Pencil,** and **Mixer Brush Tools**. Select it.

3. Now you need to take a sample of the color you want to apply to your picture. Hold the **Alt** key down and click on the eye to take the sample.

4. Then select the picture you want to retouch by clicking on its tab.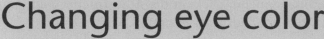

5. In the **Tools** panel, you can check if the chosen foreground color is the one you selected in the other file. 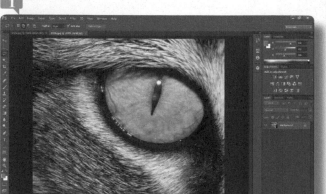 Now, you just

As you take the sample with the Color Replacement Tool, the mouse pointer takes the shape of an eyedropper.

You can also display two images at once in the work area. To do this, go to the **Window** menu, click on the **Arrange** command and select the **Tile** option.

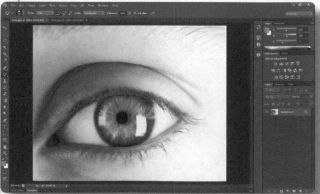

032

simply need to paint over the eye with the new color and be careful not to cover up the area of the iris. Click and drag the eye to change its color.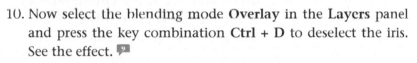

6. There is another technique, which is perhaps more complicated, but just as effective. Recover the original look of the image by using the **History** panel, and create a new layer by pressing the combination **Ctrl + J**.

7. Use the **Lasso Tool** to select the iris of the eye and apply the **Paint Bucket Tool** to fill the selection with the color you want to give the eye. (In the example you keep the same color as before, so do not worry about the initial effect).

8. Then, open the **Filter** menu, click on the **Blur** option and select **Gaussian Blur**.

9. In the **Radius** field, enter the value 7 (this is an approximate value) and click on the **OK** button.

10. Now select the blending mode **Overlay** in the **Layers** panel and press the key combination **Ctrl + D** to deselect the iris. See the effect.

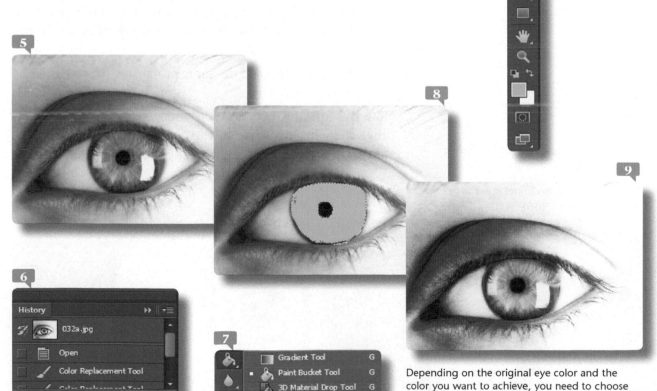

History

032a.jpg

Open

Color Replacement Tool

Gradient Tool   G
Paint Bucket Tool   G
3D Material Drop Tool   G

Depending on the original eye color and the color you want to achieve, you need to choose the right foreground color.

Adding sparkle to the eyes

IN THIS EXERCISE, YOU WILL CONTINUE TO PRACTICE how to retouch the eyes of a portrait. This time, you will brighten the eyes. This retouch can be obtained by improving the lighting conditions, so that the eyes will attract all the attention.

1. You can carry out this simple retouch on any portrait in the foreground or on sample image **033.jpg**. Once you have opened the photo in Photoshop, go to the **Filter** menu, click on the **Sharpen** command and choose the **Unsharp Mask** option.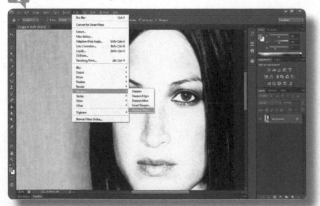

2. The **Unsharp Mask** dialog box will open, where you need to use the **Quantity**, **Radius** and the focus **Threshold** sliders based on the focus of the picture you are using. In the example, you have set a quantity of 100%, a radius of 5 pixels, and a threshold of 4 levels. You can see the effect the mask has on the image if you have the **Preview** option enabled. Once you defined the focus, click on the **OK** button to apply the filter.

3. To reapply the filter with the same properties, press **Ctrl + F** as often as necessary.

4. Now the image is over-focused and you may see noise and other elements that may distort the picture. Go to the **Unsharp Mask** panel to get back to the original image. Click on

The **Unsharp Mask** is the most used effect by professional photographers as it offers maximum control over the focus control process.

the first icon on the vertical bar, which is located on the right of the workspace, to open that panel.

5. As you know, in this panel you can see the steps you have carried out, and which should open and apply focus masks. Click on the history state **Open** to restore the picture's original appearance.

6. Now you fix the source for the **History Brush Tool** (with which you have worked with in some other exercises). Click on the box situated to the left of the last history state, **Unsharp Mask.**

7. Now select the **History Brush Tool** in the **Tools** panel (remember it is the tenth icon)).

8. Then you need to select an appropriate brush size to paint over the eye. You can do this in the **Brush Picker** in the **Options Bar.**

9. Click once on the iris of each eye and see how the brush works: the eye is painted with the color it had before Unsharp Mask was applied, while the rest of the image remains intact. Now the eyes look much brighter and attract much more attention!

10. Take advantage of having the **History** panel open and check the difference between the original and the retouched image by clicking consecutively on the states **Open** and **History Brush.**

Remember that you can also open the **History** panel from the **Window** menu.

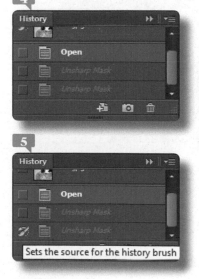

Sets the source for the history brush

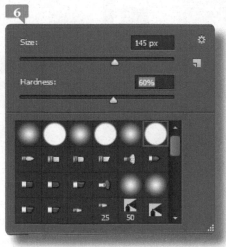

Improving the appearance of teeth

TEETH ARE RARELY BRIGHT WHITE, since it is not natural, but when they are too yellow it looks bad. With Photoshop, you can easily and quickly whiten teeth without giving them an "artificial" effect. In this exercise, you will see how.

1. To begin, open the image you would like to retouch in Photoshop (if you wish you can use sample file **034.jpg**).

2. With the help of the **Lasso Tool**, which is the third icon in the **Tools** panel, select the teeth in the image by creating a selection around them (to achieve a more precise result, you can try to increase the display zoom of the surrounding area). 🔲

3. So that you do not end up with a harsh edge when applying the bleaching effect, you need to increase the resolution of the selection. To do that, go to the **Select** menu, click on the **Modify** option and select **Feather**. 🔲

4. In the **Feather Selection** box, set a Feather Radius of **1 pixel** and click on **OK**. 🔲

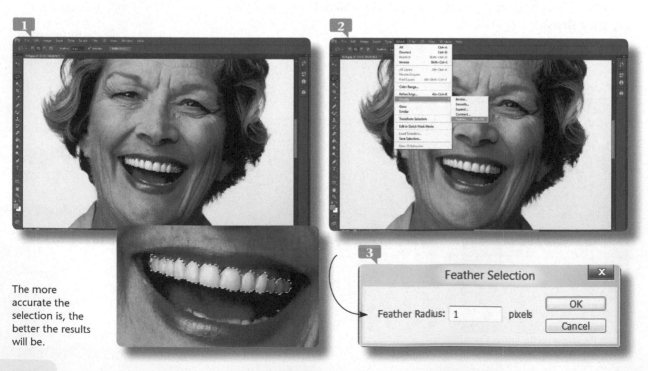

The more accurate the selection is, the better the results will be.

034

5. Add an **Hue/Saturation** adjustment layer. To do this, click on the first icon in the second row of the **Create** panel, and there you can find the **Adjustment** option preselected. [4]

6. Go to the menu that displays the **Master** option in the **Properties** panel, and select **Yellows**. [5]

7. Then, drag the **Saturation** slider to the left, in order to reduce the yellow areas of the teeth in the picture you are using. [6]

8. After the removal of the yellow of the teeth, you need to whiten them and make them shine. To do this, select the **Master** option in the **Properties** panel again and drag the **Lightness** slider to the right to get the desired effect. [7]

9. Be careful not to overdo the retouching, so that the smile does not like unnatural. Fit the entire image on the screen to check the result by opening the menu path **View/Fit on Screen**.

10. To compare the original image [8] with the retouched one, [9] show and hide the adjustment layer **Hue/Saturation**, which has been added to the **Layers** panel.

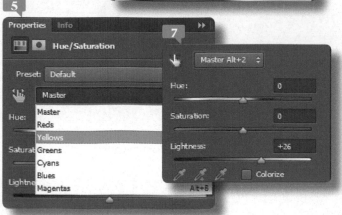

First of all, reduce the saturation of the tone you want to remove, in this case the yellow, and then add luminosity to all the colors of the image.

Removing skin shine

IN THIS LESSON WE WILL show you a simple Photoshop technique that helps you to eliminate reflections, glare, or other hot spots that can appear in a photograph. These defects are usually caused by bad lighting or flash reflections, and thereby, the subject appears to be sweating.

1. Start by opening the image you would like to retouch in Photoshop (you can use example image **035.jpg**). Apply a zoom to the image if necessary.

2. Select the **Clone Stamp Tool** in the **Tools** panel.

3. In the **Options Bar**, open the list of blending modes and select the **Darken** option, so that the modification only affects the lighter pixels rather than the area that you want to use as a sample.

4. Double-click on the **Opacity** field in the **Options Bar**, insert the value **50%** and press **Enter** to apply it.

5. Then display the **Brush Picker** and choose an appropriate brush size depending on the image you are retouching (in this case choose one of 150 pixels) and a soft tip.

The lighter pixels are, in this case, the glare and the reflections that you want to correct.

You can activate the **Clone Stamp Tool** by pressing the **S** key on your keyboard.

6. Hold the **Alt** key down and click on a point in the picture where the skin is perfect to take a sample.

7. Now you have to paint carefully the areas affected by glare. If there are hot spots in various parts of the face, as in the sample image on the forehead, nose, cheekbones, neck, and arm, you have to take good samples with a proper brush of the areas close to the bad points, so that the tone of the pixels is as close as possible. After a few clicks, your picture will have improved noticeably. If you wish you can check the result by accessing the **History** panel and display both states (the original and retouched one).

8. To finish this exercise, keep a copy of the image in its original format or save it in Photoshop's own format with the help of the **Save As** option in the **File** menu.

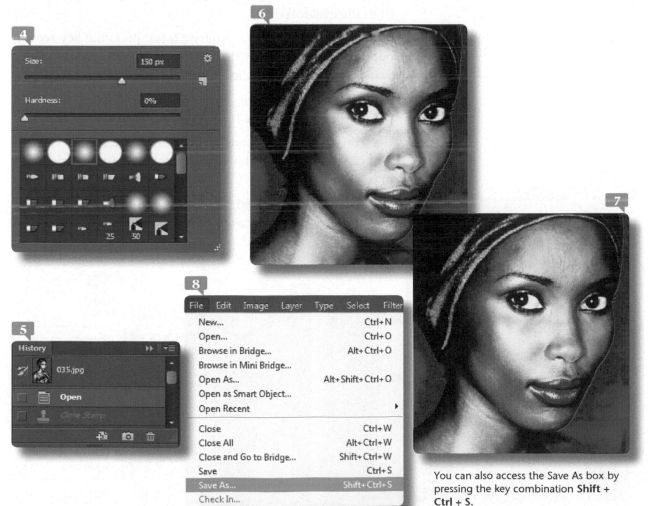

You can also access the Save As box by pressing the key combination **Shift + Ctrl + S.**

Improving eyebrows and eyelashes

THE TECHNIQUE, WHICH YOU CAN SEE BELOW, is one of the most commonly used method by professionals to improve the look of eyebrows and eyelashes in photos. This technique involves the use of so-called layer masks, on which the necessary adjustments are made.

1. Open the image you want to modify in Photoshop. (You can also use sample file **036.jpg.**)

2. Select the **Lasso Tool** and draw a selection around the eyebrow (it is not necessary to be very accurate; it can be broader than the eyebrow).

3. To put the eyebrows on a separate layer, press the key combination **Ctrl + J**. See how the new layer is added to the **Layers** panel and how it only contains the selection.

4. In the **Layers** panel, select the **Multiply** blending mode for the new layer 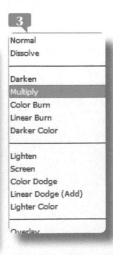 and see how the selection is darkened.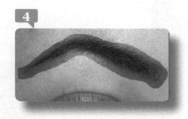

5. Hold the **Alt** key down, and click on the third icon at the bottom of the **Layers** panel, which corresponds to the **Add layer mask** icon.

6. This layer should be filled with black to hide the effect of multiplication. Select white as the foreground color.

7. Then select the **Brush Tool** in the **Brush Picker** and select a soft-tip brush in the size of the widest part of the eyebrow.

8. In the **Options Bar**, set a percentage of opacity to 50% and then paint the eyebrows. To reduce the brush size as you paint, press the chevron key (<) while dragging. **6**

9. Repeat the process to improve the look of the eyelashes. With the **Lasso Tool**, select the eye of the model and make sure to include the eyelashes. **7**

10. Move to the **Background** layer and press the key combination **Ctrl + J** to create a new layer that only includes the selection.

11. Apply the **Multiply** blending mode to the new layer and create a layer mask by clicking on the appropriate icon in combination with the **Alt** key.

12. Select white as the foreground color, **8** choose an appropriate brush and paint with it on the area of the eyelashes. Then check if the eye of the model is now more attractive and if it seems to be slightly painted. **9**

036

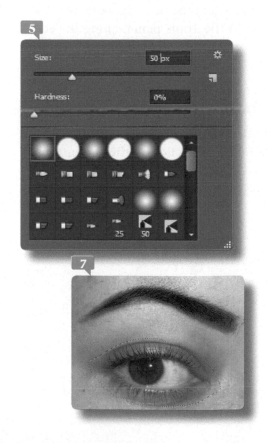

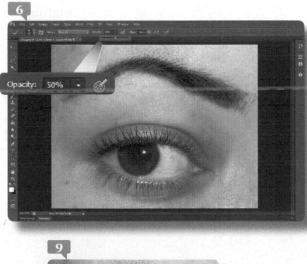

Extracting an object from its background

Learning Image retouch with Photoshop CS6 Level 2: Practical exercises

IMPORTANT

Press the **Control** key while tracing the silhouette of a person or an object you want to extract. As you click on that button, the tool automatically adapts much better to the contours and it works more accurately.

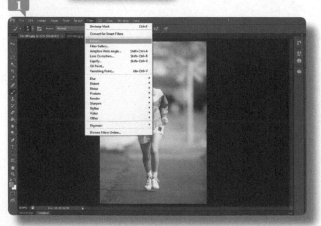

ANY INTERESTING PHOTOMONTAGE involves removing a person or object from its original position and putting it someplace else. To carry this out, there are various techniques, but some of them are more effective than others. The effectiveness is primarily based on how to treat hair details, in the case of working with people. Thanks to the Extract filter and the related subsequent adjustments, extractions can appear seamless.

1. Choose two pictures that could make for a good photomontage, so that you can extract a person from a background and place it in another image. If you prefer, you can use sample files **037-001.jpg** and **037-002.jpg**. After opening the two photos, put the person you want to extract from the background on the foreground, open the **Filter** menu and click on the **Extract** command.

2. In the **Extract** box, select the person. Drag with the Edge highlighter, the first icon in the Tools panel, along the edges of the person. (If needed, you can enlarge the image with the zoom tool in this box.)

3. After defining the subject, select the **Fill Tool** (which is represented by a paint bucket) and click on it.

4. Click on the **Preview** button to check the result of the extraction, and if this is what you wanted, click on the **OK** button.

Please know that as you carry out the extraction process, the action you are performing at any moment is displayed on the top of the Filter dialog box.

5. The person is taken from its picture and now displayed on a transparent background. To improve the appearance of the image, create a duplicate layer by pressing **Ctrl + J** and then use the **History Brush** and **Eraser Tools** to fix it. Combine both layers in the **Layers** panel by selecting them and pressing the key combination **Ctrl + E**.

6. Depending on the images you are practicing with, you may have to adjust their size so that the content of both adapt to each other. To do this, follow the path **Edit/Transform/Scale** and adjust the width and height in the appropriate fields of the Application window.

7. Now follow the menu path **Window/Arrange/Tile All Vertically** to display the two open files at once and, with the **Move Tool**, click on the left image and drag it until it reaches the desired point of the background image.

8. Check in the **Layers** panel if the image now has a new layer located above the **Background** layer, named **Layer 1**.

9. Depending on the ground, you may need to remove some of the items displayed in the image that should not be there. In this case, use the **Eraser Tool**. Then, open the Options menu of the **Layers** panel and choose **Flatten Image** to merge the two layers into one. End the exercise by closing the image you used as a background to have a look at the result.

IMPORTANT

If the **Extract** filter is not available in the gallery of filters, please download it from Adobe's official website, www.adobe.com, and add it easily to the plug-ins folder in Photoshop.

7

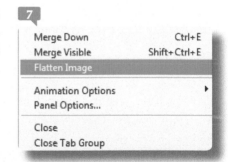

4

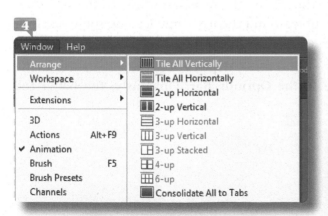

6

5

It is new in Photoshop CS6 that when you use the Move Tool, the program gives you some information about the exact location of the object in the document next to the cursor.

Moving and duplicating some elements

IN PHOTOSHOP CS6, A NEW TOOL WAS ADDED, called Content-Aware Move, which is a combination of the Clone Stamp and Patch Tools with which you can move a part of a photograph to a new location. It automatically replaces part of the image with the content interpreted by Photoshop from another part of the image. This process is very complex, but it provides surprising results, as you will see in this exercise.

1. In order to carry out this exercise, you can use sample image **038.jpg**, which you will find in the download area on our website. Once you open the image in Photoshop, select the new **Content-Aware Move** tool, which shares space in the Tools panel with the Spot Healing Brush, Healing Brush, Patch, and Red Eye Tools. 🗨1

2. Before you start to use the tool, duplicate the background layer by pressing **Ctrl + J**.

3. See if the **Move** mode is enabled in the **Options Bar** of the **Content-Aware Move Tool**, since it allows you to move the selection to a new point of the image. Then use the **Extend** mode, with which you can create duplicates of the selection. Draw a selection around the fox while leaving some pixels of space. 🗨2

4. The quality of the result depends on the adaptation mode you choose in the **Options Bar**. Obviously, the better the

038

adaptation is, the better the blending of the selection with the background will be. Open the **Adaptation** field and this time select the **Strict** option.

5. Now drag the selection to a new point of the picture and watch what happens when you release the mouse button.

6. Photoshop analyzes the background and the selection and automatically creates a copy of it at the point you have chosen. Press the key combination **Ctrl + D** to delete the selection and have a look at the better result.

7. Compare the original image with the new one while having the **Content-Aware Move Tool** displayed and hide the layer. Then keep on hiding the layer, move it to the **Background** layer and create a new duplicate using **Ctrl + J**.

8. Now select the **Extend** mode in the **Options Bar** of the Content-Aware Move Tool, which is still selected, and draw a new selection around the fox.

9. Drag the selection to another point of the image and, after releasing the mouse button, let Photoshop analyze and combine the objects. Then have a look at the result and deselect the copy of the fox by pressing the combination **Ctrl + D**.

As always, we recommend you practice this with your own pictures to experience the enormous potential of the fantastic and powerful **Content-Aware Move Tool**.

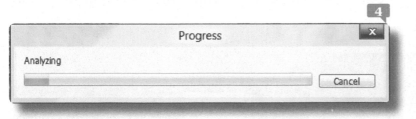

Photoshop calculates by the help of complex **algorithms**, how to fill the background as you move objects with the Content-Aware Move Tool.

Using the Unsharp Mask

ONE OF THE MISTAKES PEOPLE MAKE when taking pictures is taking blurry ones. This blurring can either be light (in this case the only solution is to smoothen the edges around the image) or heavy (due to incorrect use of the zoom when shooting). One of the techniques used in Photoshop to solve blur problems is to apply the Unsharp Mask filter, which allows you to create a focused version of the photo, which can be used like a mask on the original photo.

1. This exercise requires a slightly blurred image. If you have a picture with this problem, please use it. If not, we recommend using sample file **039.jpg**. Open the image you want to retouch, click on the **View** menu and select the **Actual Pixels** option.

2. Go to the **Filter** menu, click on the **Sharpen** command and select **Unsharp Mask** of the submenu.

3. In the **Unsharp Mask** box (which you have worked with in a previous exercise), adjust the percentage of focus, the number of pixels that should affect the focus, the difference between the pixels of the surrounding area before it is considered to be an edge pixel and focus it with the help of the filter. Drag

To display the image with its current amount of pixels, you can also press the key combination **Ctrl +1**.

039

the **Amount** slider to get an approximate value of **125%** (of course, this value can be higher or lower depending on the degree of blur in your image) and then set the Radius to **0.5 pixels.**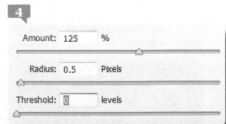

4. If the image you're working with is a close-up, the Radius value can be set to 2. If, on the other hand, the photo you want to repair is a landscape or was taken outdoors, then the best value is usually 0.5. Higher Radius values are suitable for clearly blurred photographs. In the case of large images and close-ups, it is necessary to apply a value of 4 or 5. In the **Threshold** field, insert, in this case, the value 0.

5. The values of the **Threshold** field are perhaps the most difficult to define. In images in which the subject of focus has a gentle nature, such as a flower, an animal, or a person, a Threshold value of approximately 10 is recommended. For the focus of close-ups and for a maximum focus, we suggest a Threshold of 3 pixels. In those images in which the focus is moderate (houses or landscapes), the Threshold value must be 0. Click on **OK** to apply the Unsharp Mask on the image and display it on the screen to check the final result.

6. Compare the original image with the retouched one by using the status snapshots of the **History** panel.

Because this technique involves the use of fixed values, we recommend you practice with all kinds of blurred pictures until you have fully understood the function of the parameters that have an impact on the process.

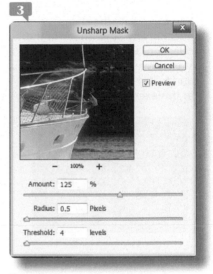

If the **Preview** option of the **Unsharp Mask** box is activated, you can check the settings directly on the image.

Creating a print effect

IMPORTANT

You can create the stamp effect in any other shape of the selection. For example, draw a star, convert it to the selection, and follow the steps indicated in this exercise.

You already know that if the selection does not satisfy you, you can undo it by pressing the key combination **Ctrl + D** and redraw it.

IN THIS EXERCISE WE WILL SHOW you a simple technique to convert a photograph into a beautiful print in which a point of unfocused light illuminates a particular part of it. This is a very popular retouch among portrait and wedding photographers, since it applies a soft light effect on the subject while its surroundings remain unaffected.

1. As you know, you can use your own image or sample **040.jpg**. Once you open the picture in Photoshop, select the **Elliptical Marquee Tool** in the **Tools** panel 🔽 and create a selection frame at the point of the image that you would like to highlight. 🔽

2. Add a new layer to the document by clicking on the icon **Create a new layer** in the **Layers** panel. 🔽

3. In order to convert the elliptical selection into a layer mask, hold the **Alt** key down while clicking on the **Add layer mask** icon, which is the third icon in the **Layers** panel. 🔽

4. Have a look at the panel. Indeed, a layer mask has been added to the black selection. Select the thumbnail of **layer 1**, set

If you hold down the **Alt** key, you can create a layer mask that fills with black.

040

black as the foreground color, 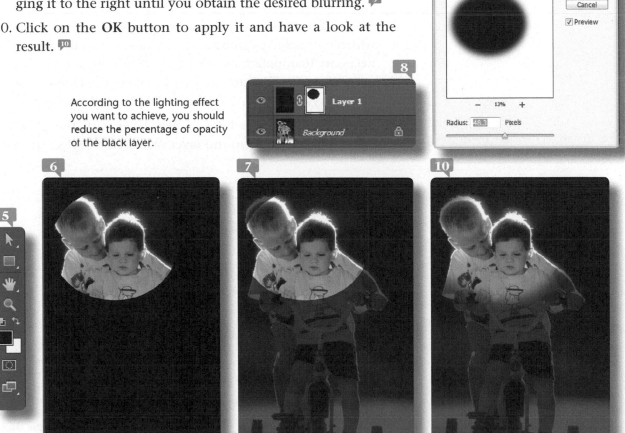 and press the key combination **Alt + Delete** to fill the layer with that color.

5. There is an immediate effect. A light seems to illuminate the selection while the rest of the image is displayed in black. You need to mitigate the effect of the lighting. Reduce the opacity of the selected layer until the image shows the lighting effect you prefer.

6. Then, you need to take the selection ellipse out of focus slightly in order to add further nuance to the print effect. In the Layers panel, select the thumbnail of the layer mask, which is the one that includes the black ellipse.

7. Go to the **Filter** menu, click on the **Blur** option and select the **Gaussian Blur** option.

8. In the **Gaussian Blur** box, use the icons + and – until the elliptical selection is displayed as completed in the preview.

9. Then drag the slider all the way to the left and keep on dragging it to the right until you obtain the desired blurring.

10. Click on the **OK** button to apply it and have a look at the result.

According to the lighting effect you want to achieve, you should reduce the percentage of opacity of the black layer.

Focusing extreme close-ups

IT SOMETIMES HAPPENS THAT, WHILE TAKING CLOSE-UPS, the resulting image does not have the sharpness it should have, since there is blurring in the photograph. Thanks to the edge sharpening technique, it is possible to largely smooth the edges of areas with less sharpness, thus providing depth and a greater amount of relief. This technique can be used for any type of photographs, because it is not just limited to extreme close-ups. Thus, the focus of edges is a good technique for images that require a very high level of focus.

1. For this exercise, you can use an own image that provides the specified characteristics, or sample image **041.jpg**. In any case, open the image you would like to retouch in the Photoshop workspace.

2. As you already know, the picture opens with a single layer, which is called **Background**,  and you need to introduce the necessary manipulations on a duplicate of this layer. To begin, press the key combination **Ctrl + J** or go to the Options menu of the **Layers** panel and select the **Duplicate Layer** option.

3. Following both procedures, a new layer with the identical content of the **Background** layer is created. 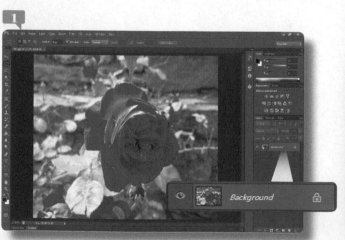 Select the new

To **rename** the layer, double-click on it, type in the new name and press the Enter key.

layer, go to the **Filter** menu, click on the **Stylize** command and select the **Emboss** option from the submenu. **3**

4. In the **Emboss** dialog box, configure the values needed to apply greater depth to the image edges. By default, the **Angle** and **Amount** parameters display 135 and 100 respectively. Normally, these values can be maintained as they are, but it is necessary to adjust the value corresponding to the height. Double-click on the **Height** field, enter an approximate value of **3** pixels and click on **OK** to apply the filter. **4**

5. The image has been tinted gray while at the same time the edges became colored. Do not worry, because you have more to do to achieve the desired result. In the **Layers** panel, open the list of blending modes and select the **Hard Light** option. **5**

6. Thus, the layer has regained its original color and is much more focused. If the focus is too intense, simply reduce the layer opacity to obtain the best result. **6**

When you apply the **Emboss** filter, the image is shown in gray with the edges selected in color as you can see it in the preview of the image.

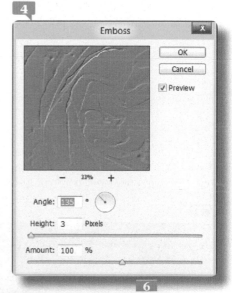

As you apply the **Hard light** blending mode to the duplicate layer, the gray gets removed and the edges are more accentuated, and thus, the perception of focus increases.

Focusing with layers

IN A PAST EXERCISE WE MENTIONED THAT if the setting of the focus quantity in an image is too high, especially when it is very out of focus, an unaesthetic digital noise may be produced. To avoid this problem, it is best to use the technique described in this exercise, which mixes different filters.

IMPORTANT

When you apply the **Color** blending mode to the blurred layer, you need to enlarge the areas that should include halos or any other color changes with the help of the zoom, and you will see that they have disappeared.

1. In this exercise we will show you how to focus a picture based on the use of layers and filters. If you have an image that displays a close-up with shaded areas and a slight blur, you can use it to carry out this exercise. In this exercise, you will use sample image **042.jpg**, which can be found in the download area on our website. Open the image in Photoshop and duplicate the background layer. To do this, press the key combination **Ctrl + J**. 1️⃣

2. Then, in the **Layers** panel, select as a blending mode the **Lighten** option. 2️⃣

3. Furthermore, apply Unsharp Mark to the new layer. Open the **Filter** menu, click on the **Sharpen** command and select the **Unsharp Mask** option.

Using layers to improve the focus in an image is best for close-up images, in which you can discern the shaded and dark areas, which are the sensitive zone in which digital noise can occur.

4. According to the image you are working with, you need to adjust the mode or the values of the filter's parameters. Move the sliders of each parameter, and when you think that you have set the Unsharp Mask correctly, press the **OK** button to apply. 3

5. The next step is to create a copy of this new layer, which, if you remember, is already duplicated. Press the key combination **Ctrl + J**.

6. On the new layer, which appears in the **Layers** panel, you have to apply a new filter. Open the **Filter** menu, click on the Blur command and select the filter **Gaussian Blur**. 4

7. This filter produces a blur that hides any sign of digital noise. In the **Radius** field, enter an appropriate value to generate a slight blur on the image and click on the **OK** button to apply the filter. 5

8. The next step is to maintain the characteristics of the applied filter, which is to conceal the noise in the image while eliminating the generated blur. To do this, open the list of blending modes in the **Layers** panel and select the **Color** option. 6

9. Open the Options menu of the **Layers** panel and click on the **Flatten image** command. Now the picture only consists of one layer called **Background**. 7

As you apply the **Gaussian blur**, any halo or digital noise will be hidden.

Blurring to draw attention

IN THIS EXERCISE YOU WILL GET TO KNOW a technique that is primarily used to emphasize and highlight a specific part of a picture. This technique is similar to the one mentioned in the section of creating prints, but in this case, it focuses on the blur of the unimportant areas and not on the "illumination" of the important areas.

1. For this exercise, you can use one of your own images, which displays one or two people in the foreground. The idea is to focus on the protagonists of the picture and leave the other parts of the photograph in a blurred condition. (If you want, you can use sample image **043.jpg**). Open the image in Photoshop, double-click on the key combination **Ctrl + J** to obtain two duplicates of the **Background** layer.

2. To hide **Layer 1 copy**, click on the visibility icon in the **Layers** panel and select the one that corresponds to that layer (remember that it is the icon that looks like an eye).

3. Enable **Layer 1** by clicking on it in the **Layers** panel.

4. The next step is to apply the Gaussian Blur to this layer. Open the **Filter** menu, click on the **Blur** option and choose **Gaussian Blur**.

5. The Filter box, which you already know well, will open. Increase the value in the **Radius** field by dragging its slider to the right until the image is noticeably blurred, and click on the **OK** button. 5

6. Redisplay **Layer 1 copy** by clicking on its visibility icon to enable it. 6

7. Select the **Elliptical Tool** in the **Tools** panel and draw an ellipse on the part you want to keep focused. 7

8. Open the **Select** menu, click on the **Modify** option and select **Feather** to soften the selection.

9. In the **Feather Radius** field, enter an approximate value of **50** pixels and click on **OK**. 8

10. Now you need to convert the selection into a layer mask to you automatically obtain the effect you wanted: the center of the image will be in focus and the other parts of the picture will be blurred. Click on the **Add layer mask** icon, which is the third icon in the **Layers** panel, and have a look at the great result. 9

11. If you wish, you can complete the exercise by attaching the image to the Options menu of the **Layers** panel and save it in your images folder.

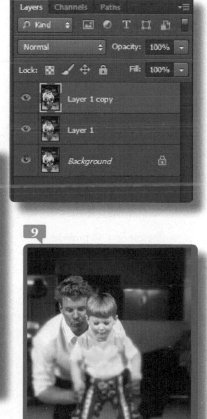

Blurring selections

IN PHOTOSHOP CS6, NEW BLUR FILTERS have been added, which expand the gallery and allow you to obtain spectacular results. The filter of selective Gaussian Blur, called Field Blur, allows you to focus on a part of a scene while keeping other parts of the same scene unfocused. Furthermore, with the help of the Iris Blur filter you can create circular and oval areas of blur, and with the Tilt-Shift filter you can fake the layout effect of a large-format camera.

1. For this exercise, in which you will practice with the three new blur filters, you can use example image **044.jpg**, which can be found in the download area of our website. Once you have opened it in Photoshop, duplicate the Background layer by pressing the combination **Ctrl + J**.

2. Now go to the **Filter** menu, click on the **Blur** option and select the new filter, **Field Blur.**

3. Then, the entire image is automatically blurred, but the controls of the **Blur Tools** tab allow you to limit the blur to specific areas. The placeholder, appearing in the image, can be dragged to any point. Place it on the child's nose.

4. To gradually set the amount of blur, use the Blur slider in the **Field Blur** box.

5. Click on the arrow tip of the **Iris Blur** box and increase the

Blur Tools

Field Blur

Blur: 35 px

To **disable** this type of blur, click on the corresponding checkbox.

Photoshop CS6 provides three new blur filters: **Field Blur, Iris Blur,** and **Tilt-Shift.**

amount to about **50 pixels**.

6. By usaging of the drawing tools, which are located in the circle that appears on the image, you can change the picture's size and shape. Furthermore, with the help of the squared drawing tool you can convert the circle into a square and with the round drawing tools you can change the image's dimensions and convert it into an ellipse. Try it!

7. Now you need to display the **Tilt-Shift** filter options.

8. With this filter, you can adjust the amount of blur by creating areas with horizontal lines that can be dragged. You can change the position of these lines by clicking on them and dragging them as the mouse pointer changes into a curved arrow when you place them in the central drawing tools. In the **Blur Tools** panel, set the blur to about **10 pixels** and the distortion of 0% and tilt the lines as in the image.

9. When you obtain the desired result, apply the filter by clicking on the **OK** button in the **Options Bar** and compare the Background layer with the Layer 1 to verify the effect.

IMPORTANT

To remove the **placeholders** of the blur in the image, click on the curved arrow icon in the Options Bar of the new filters.

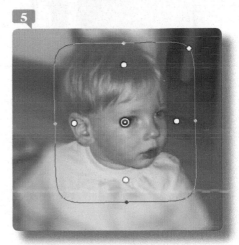

With white circles inside the focus area, you can change the radius of the blur.

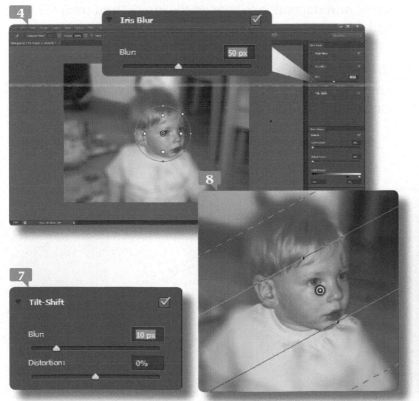

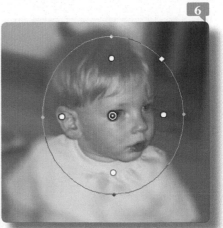

Coloring objects in black and white

IMPORTANT

If you want to choose the color you want to give the objects in a black and white image, select the Lasso Tool and create a Color Balance adjustment layer with the tonality you want to apply.

ANOTHER VERY INTERESTING TECHNIQUE OF PHOTOGRAPH-IC retouching is the one we are about to show you in this exercise, which is used to emphasize certain parts of an image. Furthermore, it refers to the coloring of certain objects or parts of a black and white image. To carry out this technique, you need a colored image. The procedure begins with the conversion of the colored image into a black and white one. In fact, this technique tries to restore the original colors of certain parts of the image after carrying out the conversion.

1. You can use any colored digital photograph that you think might be appropriate, or you can use sample image **045.jpg**. Your aim is to apply color only to one part of the image. To begin, open the image you want to retouch in the Photoshop workspace.

2. The first step you need to carry out, and as already mentioned in the introduction, is to convert the image from color to black and white. To do this, open the **Image** menu, click on the **Adjustments** command and select the **Desaturate** option. 🔲

3. Now the image has converted into a black and white image. 🔲 Then you need to color the object you want to highlight. Please note that the colors available to color are the original

045

ones of the photograph, so do not expect to choose new colors in this process. Select the **History Brush Tool**, which is the tenth icon in the **Tools** panel.

4. Depending on the object or image you want to color, choose the most adequate brush size with a soft tip in the Options Bar.

5. Now you can start to paint. (You may need to enlarge the display zoom of the chosen area). Drag the mouse over the object you want to highlight in the image, so that the original colors gradually appear.

6. If necessary, decrease or increase the brush size depending on the areas that need color. When the retouching is finished, save the document in Photoshop's own format.

This is a technique widely used in books for weddings, communions, or events in general, since it gives the photographs an elegant, original, and fresh look. We recommend you try this on various images as many times as you want in order to see the wonderful contrast that occurs when applying this technique.

Select the diameter of the history brush according to the elements of the photograph you want to color again.

This method, which is used to color objects in a black and white photograph, is perhaps the most widely accepted technique by advertisers and other professionals due to its fast usage and the concealment of possible errors.

Giving a sense of motion

SOME PHOTOGRAPHIC TECHNIQUES capture the feeling of motion by producing an out of focus of the background of an image in contrast to the foreground. This exercise describes in detail the process of how to add this sense of movement to a completely focused image. This technique is suitable for images in which you can see someone moving and which have been taken with the appropriate exposure settings that support any sensation of movement: a running animal, a moving vehicle, a person playing sports, etc.

1. If you do not have any pictures of moving people or things, use example image **046.jpg**. To begin, open the image in the Photoshop workspace.

2. The following process requires the creation of a layer mask, so you need to duplicate the **Background** layer, since it is not possible to modify its specific aspects. Press the key combination **Ctrl + J.** 1

3. Then, you need to apply a motion filter. To do this, open the **Filter** menu, click on the **Blur** command and select the **Motion Blur** option. 2

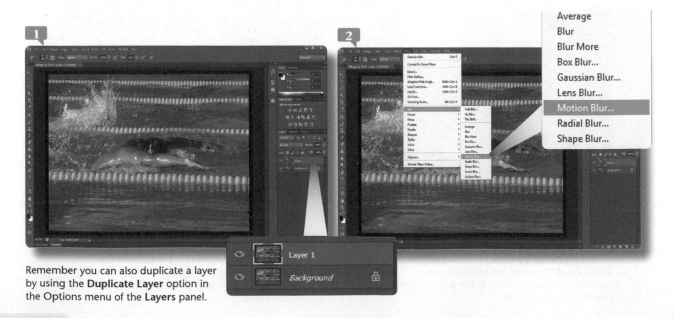

Remember you can also duplicate a layer by using the **Duplicate Layer** option in the Options menu of the **Layers** panel.

4. The filter is applied to the image, and blurs it according to some default parameters: the angle, which indicates the direction from which the blur is applied, and the distance, which sets the amount of blur. The angle should be fixed due to the assumption that the displacement is horizontal, vertical, or diagonal. In this case, as the movement is horizontal, you can leave the value of the field **Angle** as 0 degrees. 3

5. As for the distance, increase or decrease its amount until you obtain a blur of motion that suits the type of subject or object of the image. After carrying out the necessary adjustments, press the **OK** button to apply the filter.

6. The background is also blurred and this problem can be solved the following way. Create a layer mask. Then press the **Alt** key without releasing it, and click on the icon **Add layer mask** at the bottom of the **Layers** panel. 4

7. The layer mask fills with black 5 and hides the effect of motion. You can only restore the moving foreground. Enable the **Brush Tool** in the **Tools** panel and, in the **Options Bar**, select a medium-sized brush according to the area that needs movement.

8. Choose white as the foreground color by pressing the **X** key 6 and paint, by dragging, the subject or object of the photo to which you want to add movement (normally, the blurring is applied to the posterior area).

When you are finished with the retouching, hide Layer 1 to compare the resulting image with the original one.

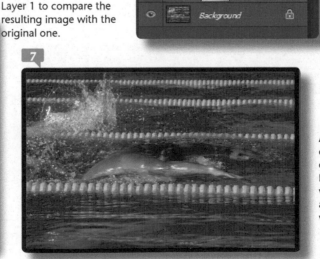

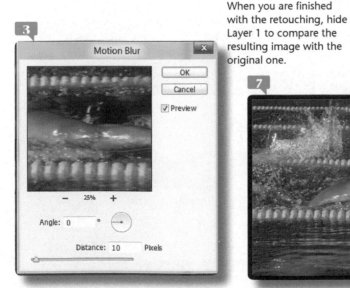

As you paint concrete parts of the image, Motion Blur, which has been assigned earlier, will be displayed.

Adding warmth to an image

MANY PHOTOGRAPHERS USE THE COLOR correction filters 81A and 81B to add warmer tones to their photographs. They are especially used in photographs that were either taken outdoors on days with blue sky or on sunny days in the shade or on cloudy days. As a consequence, those photos take on a bluish hue.

1. In this exercise, we will show you how to reproduce the color correction filters 81A and 81B in Photoshop. You will need a photograph taken under the conditions described in the introduction. (If you do not have any, you can use our sample file, **047.jpg**). After opening the image, you can access the Warming Filter from the **Adjustments** mode of the new **Create** panel, or from the Fill layer icon or from the adjustment of the **Layers** panel. This time, click on the fourth icon in the second row of the **Create** panel, which corresponds to the **Photo Filter** option.

2. The parameters of the filters of the image are also displayed in the new **Properties** panel. As you can see, by default Photoshop applies Warming Filter (85),  which changes significantly the tone of the image. Display the filter list and select **Warming Filter (81)**.

047

3. By default, Photoshop also applies a Density filter value of 25%, which is perhaps too soft. Drag the Density slider to the right until about **45%**. Then you can see how the effect is carried out.

4. In photographs with people in it, you can now see that especially the flesh tones appear warmer. You can restore the original state of certain areas in the photograph with the help of the **Brush Tool**. Enable it in the **Tools** panel.

5. Select an appropriate brush size out of the brush selector in the **Options Bar**. The brush size should depend on the area to which you want to restore the original tone. Select black as the foreground color.

6. Now you just need to paint the areas you do not want to filter. Since the filter has been applied as a configurable adjustment layer, you just need to paint on this layer in order to see the original Background layer. Compare the original image with the retouched one by hiding and redisplaying the **Photo Filter 1** layer.

The higher the percentage of **Density** applied to the filter of the photograph, the more evident the effects on the image will be.

Note that the layer **mask thumbnail** in the Layers panel is displayed as you paint with the black brush on the image.

Changing the color of an object

IT IS VERY COMMON THAT A PHOTOGRAPHER'S clients change their minds at the last minute, and want to change something in an image. For example, they do not like the color of a tie or they want to reduce the intensity of the flower that they are wearing. With Photoshop it is very quick and easy to make these color changes.

1. Open an image that contains an object whose color you want to change. (You can also use sample file **048.jpg**).

2. First you need to select the area in which you want to change the color. To carry this out, you can use the selection tools **Lasso, Pen, Magic Wand, Rectangular Marquee, Elliptical Marque,** etc. Remember that if the **Add to selection** option in the **Options Bar** is enabled (or if you press the **Shift** key and select it again), the new selections are added to the first one. If you are working with the sample image, select the **Magic Wand Tool** in the **Tools** panel ▣ and, after setting the Tolerance in the **Options Bar** to a value of **45 pixels,** ▣ keep on clicking on the guard's uniform in the foreground until it is completely selected. ▣

| Point Sample | Tolerance: 45 | ✓ Anti-alias |

You can activate the tool from the keyboard by clicking on the **W** key.

Change the **Tolerance** and the modes of **addition** and **deletion** of the Magic Wand Tool to select the whole uniform.

048

3. Select the part whose color you want to change, and click on the first icon in the second row of the **Create** panel, which corresponds to the **Hue/Saturation** adjustment.

4. This creates a new adjustment layer of the selected type. Enable the **Colorize** option in the **Properties** panel of this setting.

5. Now you just need to choose a color in the **Hue** slider and change the Saturation values and brightness if necessary.

6. Increase the saturation of the selected color by dragging the regulator of the **Saturation** field to the right.

7. To darken the color tone, drag the Lightness slider slightly to the left and watch how the object changes.

8. With a few steps, you have changed the color of an object perfectly. Go to the **History** panel and revise the change with the help of two steps: click on **Open** and then on **Modify Hue/ Saturation Layer.**

9. Close the **History** panel and if you want to, you can keep a copy of the modified image in the Photoshop format by clicking on the menu path **File/Save As.**

Move the sliders **Hue, Saturation,** and **Lightness** of the **Hue/Saturation** settings until you get the desired color for your image.

Making a photo collage

THE FOLLOWING TECHNIQUE, WHICH we will show you, is one of the most popular one among professionals since it is a quick and easy way to create perfectly merged photo collages.

1. This time you will merge three photos to create a collage. As always, you can use sample files **049-001.jpg**, **049-002.jpg**, and **049-003.jpg** or choose your own photographs. To begin, open the image that is going to serve as the background of the collage (in this case, **049-001**).

2. Then open the first photo you want to add to the collage (in this case, **049-002**).

3. Use the menu path **Window/Arrange/Tile All Vertically**  to display an image next to the other one and drag the second picture with the help of the **Move Tool** and place it on the one which will be the background.

4. Close the second image and move the second layer of the first document to the right.

5. Click on the third icon at the bottom of the **Layers** panel which corresponds to the option **Add Layer Mask**.

In order to obtain a result of perfect fusion and without any image border, it is desirable that all the images have the same height.

You can enlarge the canvas size, if necessary, by accessing the **Canvas Size** dialog box in the **Image** menu.

6. Select the **Gradient** tool from the **Tools** panel, 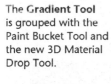 open the gradient picker in the **Options Bar** and select with a double-click on the third one (from black to white).

7. Click on the intersection of the two photos and drag it almost an inch to the right to create the gradient effect. Watch how the two images start to merge.

8. Now open the third image you want to add to the collage (sample image, **048-003**).

9. You need to repeat the first steps. Display the segmented images and, with the help of the **Move Tool**, drag the third image and place it on the background of the collage.

10. Close the third image and place it wherever you want in the background photo.

11. To add a layer mask to this new layer, click on the third icon at the bottom of the **Layers** panel.

12. Reapply the black to white gradient to create the merging effect for the images (if you have placed the image on the left of the background image, click on the intersection and drag it with the **Gradient Tool** to the left).

13. Reduce the opacity of the layers added to the background to achieve an effect you like.

049

IMPORTANT

As you click on the layer while applying a gradient, the top layer becomes transparent and the slider stops at 100% opacity. Change the different orientations of the gradient and have a look at the different effects you can achieve.

Change the **opacity** of the layers and the application of **gradients** to obtain spectacular effects on the collage.

The **Gradient Tool** is grouped with the Paint Bucket Tool and the new 3D Material Drop Tool.

Gradient Tool	G
Paint Bucket Tool	G
3D Material Drop Tool	G

Black, White

You can also use other gradient types to achieve different merging effects in your images.

You can also apply **Blur** and other filters to one of the images to improve the result even more.

Fixing Keystoning issues

THE KEYSTONING EFFECT OCCURS WHEN the surface of a photographed building and the image of the camera are not parallel to each other, which causes the illusion of a conversion of the building sides. Although the keystoning effect can sometimes have artistic purposes, it can also cause a somewhat strange effect depending on how the image was taken. Photoshop can eliminate this effect. All you have to do is to perform the steps in this exercise.

1. For this exercise you need a photograph in which this effect occurs. If you do not have any, you can use sample file **050.jpg**. In any case, open the photo you want to retouch in the Photoshop workspace.

2. As always, you need to create a duplicate of the Background layer so that you can carry out the changes on the new layer without any difficulties. To do this, press the key combination **Ctrl + J.**

3. To perform this technique, it is essential that you can view the entire image on the screen. Do this by choosing **Fit on Screen** from the **View** menu.

You can also fit the image on the screen by pressing the key combination **Ctrl +0.**

4. Another requirement, which is almost essential to correct the keystoning effect more easily, is to use a grid: you will obtain a sequence of vertical references to 90 degrees, which will help you to find out which sides of the building are completely straight. To display this Photoshop item, go to the **View** menu, click on the **Show** command and select the **Grid** option.

5. After making these adjustments, you can start with the process itself. Open the **Edit** menu, click on the **Transform** command and select the **Perspective** option.

6. At the image borders you can now see some sliders as well as a signal in the center of the picture. For now, you do not need to modify any of the parameters of the **Options Bar**. What you should do is drag the sliders surrounding the image to obtain a proper perspective.

7. As you use the **Perspective** command for the first time, it is very likely that you find it a bit difficult to achieve the right fit. Practice is very important, so do not hesitate to repeat this process again and again until you obtain the best correction. When you have finished, click on the **Commit Transform** icon which is located at the very right end of the **Options Bar**, which is symbolized by a check mark.

8. Hide the grid by following the menu path **View/Show/Grid** and have a look at the result.

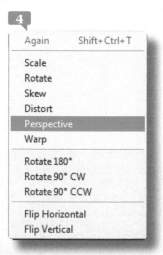

If you display the grid of the **View** menu, it will be much easier for you to correct the image perspective.

Change the sliders, by dragging them, until you obtain the proper perspective.

Correcting crooked images

IF YOU TAKE IMAGES WITHOUT USING A TRIPOD and hold the camera in your hands, it is very common the photographs will be are a little crooked. This exercise will show you how to straighten them in a few easy steps.

1. As always, you can use your own image, which should be slightly crooked, or sample image **051.jpg**. Once opened in Photoshop, select the **Ruler Tool**, which is grouped with the **Eyedropper**, **3D Material Eyedropper**, **Color Sampler**, **Note**, and **Count Tools** in the **Tools** panel.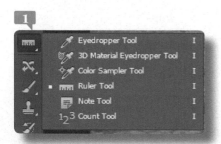

2. By clicking and dragging, draw a line on an area of the image you think isn't horizontal (in our image you will select the bottom of the image, which has a slight upward incline).

3. In the **Options Bar** of the **Ruler Tool** you can find the angle of inclination of the line you have drawn. The next step is to rotate the canvas based on the angle obtained in the measurement. Go to the **Image** menu, click on the **Image Rotation** command and select the **Arbitrary** option.

4. This opens the **Rotate Canvas** dialog box, which displays in the **Angle** field the necessary inclination value to straighten

You can activate the **Ruler Tool** by pressing the key combination **Shift + L**.

051

the image (based on the measurement) and the enabled **°CW** option (which means clockwise). Keep this setting and click on the **OK** button.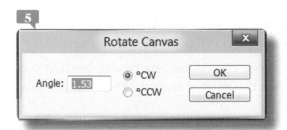

5. The picture is automatically straightened and corrected. You can check this by drawing a line with the **Ruler Tool** right under the boat and make sure that the inclination angle in the **Options Bar** is 0°. Now you have to crop the image to remove the blank spaces that have appeared after the straightening. Enable the **Crop Tool** in the **Tools** panel.

6. Draw, by dragging, the crop area so that it does not include any blank areas and approve the cut by clicking on the icon **Commit current crop operation**, which is symbolized by a checkmark in the **Options Bar**.

7. Note that it is possible to automatically straighten a photograph by using the menu path **File/Automate/Crop and Straighten Photos**. This creates a duplicate of the straightened image in a separate document.

You can also confirm the cut by pressing the Enter key on your keyboard.

This option is very useful to straighten and separate scanned photos in documents.

Removing objects or people

PHOTOSHOP PROVIDES A GREAT TOOL with which you can delete objects or people in the background of an image. The Fill command, which can be found in the Edit menu of the application, substitutes in its Content-Aware mode the eliminated element with a content that blends perfectly into the given environment.

1. In this exercise, you will discover the new **Fill** command, with which you can delete items from an image. We recommend using sample files **052-001.jpg** and **052-002.jpg**. Open the first image in Photoshop and select the **Quick Selection Tool**, which is grouped with the **Magic Wand Tool** in the **Tools** panel. 🔲

2. Adjust the size of the tool and the tolerance and select the dog. 2️⃣

3. Now you have selected the item you want to delete. To do this, go to the **Edit** menu and click on the **Fill** command. 3️⃣

4. In the **Fill** dialog box you can choose the type of content you want to use to replace the deleted item. In the example, you

You can also access the **Fill** command with the key combination **Shift + F5**.

052

should focus on the existing background. Note that, depending on what you want to achieve, you can use the functions of the program to refill the selected area, apply background and foreground colors or any other color by selecting them in the **Use field** of this box. Further, do not modify the Contents, Blending Mode, and Opacity, and click on **OK** to have a look at the result. 4

5. The dog disappears and the empty space is automatically filled with the current background color. Press the key combination **Ctrl + D** to delete the selection and look at the result. 5

6. Then open sample image **052-002.jpg**. Now you want to remove the person from the image. Use the new **Quick Selection Tool** to select the silhouette of the person. 6

7. Open the **Fill** dialog box in the **Edit** menu, keep the settings, and press the **OK** button.

8. The process can take a bit longer, since it depends on the amount of information that Photoshop needs to process. 7 The result is that the person in the image disappears. 8 If there are areas that remain or which display small imperfections, you can use the **Healing Brush** and **Spot Healing Brush Tools** to eliminate them. 9

Distorting parts of an image

IMPORTANT

To remove a location you need to select it and click on the **Delete Pin** command in its context menu. You can also remove locations if you place the cursor directly over them, and hold down the **Alt** key as the cursor turns into scissors.

Delete Pin
Set Auto Rotation
Reset Depth

THE PUPPET WARP COMMAND was a new addition to Photoshop CS5.1 and provides a visual mesh with which you can distort certain areas in an image without affecting the other parts.

1. To carry out this exercise, you can use your own image or sample file **053.jpg**. In any case, open the photo in the Photoshop workspace.

2. In the example image, you want to change the fabric. In order to perform the change, you first need to select the part you are interested in. To do this, simply click on the **Magic Wand Tool** in the **Tools** panel.

3. Then, adjust the Tolerance and the Brush sizes, and click on the red fabric to select it completely.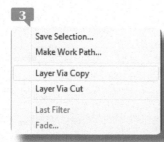

4. Click with the right mouse button on the selected item in the picture and select the **Layer Via Copy** option in the context menu.

5. Check that a new layer with the selected item appears in the Layers panel. Let's start the transformation process. Make sure that the new layer is selected, go to the **Edit** menu and click on the **Puppet Warp** option.

Save Selection...
Make Work Path...
Layer Via Copy
Layer Via Cut
Last Filter
Fade...

053

6. Note that the program covers the selected object with a mesh. This mesh can be adjusted in the **Options Bar**. Display the **Mode** field and select the **Distort** option.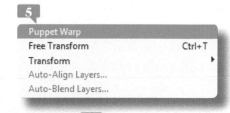

7. This option also allows you to change the shape of the element, not just rotate it. The **Density** and **Expansion** fields and the **Show Mesh** option allow you to configure the shape of the mesh. Moreover, the **Pin Depth** option is used to overlay new meshes with the existing ones. The **Rotate** field is activated as you insert the locations in the image. It is common to define three points along the area you want to retouch. In this case, insert three points at the bottom of the image by clicking on them while holding down the **Shift** key.

8. Then define another location at the very right of the fabric without releasing the mouse button, and drag it down. 7

9. From here on, freely distort the selected area until you obtain the desired result. Now your creativity and your skills are needed to carry out this command. As you have finished, click on the **Commit Puppet Warp** command, which is last icon in the **Options Bar**, 8 and have a look at the final result.

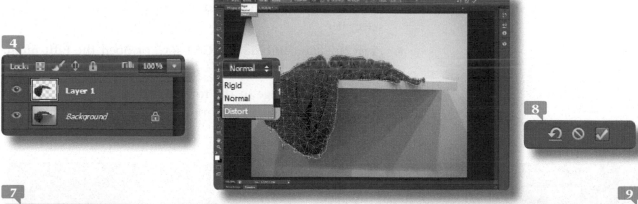

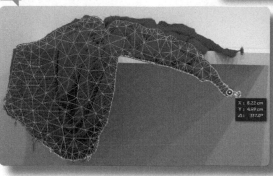

New to Photoshop CS6 is that as you move the cursor, you can see the coordinates and inclination angle of the displacement.

Changing the sky in an image

SOMETIMES WHEN YOU TAKE PICTURES with a digital camera, you realize that it would have been better if the sky had been cloudy or, on the contrary, bright blue. This exercise includes two techniques with which you can change the color of the sky. The first one involves using various photographs, and the second one makes use of the Clouds filter.

1. We recommend using sample files **054-001.jpg** and **054-002. jpg**. The first technique consists of a simple substitution of the skies. Place image **054-001.jpg** in the foreground and select the **Magic Warp Tool** in the **Tools** panel.

2. Click on the sky of the image to select it (remember that, with the help of the **Shift** key, you can add areas that, due to their color, are not included in the initial selection).

3. Place file **054-002** in the foreground, which displays a different sky as the first image. Go to the **Select** menu and select the **All** option. (If you use an image in which the sky is not the absolute content, you should use one of the selection tools to select it.)

4. Press the key combination **Ctrl + C**, or open the **Edit** menu and select **Copy**.

5. Place the first image in the foreground again, go to the **Edit** menu, click on the **Paste** option and select the **Paste Into**

command to add the copied areas to the selected area. [3]

6. The replacement was carried out without any problems. [4] The second process described in this exercise uses a single photograph, and it involves the usage of the **Clouds** filter. This time, it does not matter if you utilize the image provided with this book or if you use your own photograph to retouch the sky by applying a cloak of clouds. If you choose to use our sample image, press the key combination **Ctrl + Z** to undo the bonding of the sky and restore your selection.

7. The **Clouds** filter, included in the **Render** category, applies a layer of clouds by using the selected colors for the foreground and background of the **Tools** panel. If these colors are black and white or vice versa, the aspect of the picture with the new sky will be the one of a gray day. Choose a blue tone as a background color.

8. Open the **Filter** menu, click on the **Render** category and select the **Clouds** option. [5]

9. The change is immediately carried out and spectacularly so. Press the key combination **Ctrl + D** to delete the selection of the image. [6]

054

Use the **Move Tool** to place the background image in the position you like most. [4]

Converting an image into an old one

IN THIS LESSON WE WILL SHOW YOU A SIMPLE technique that allows you to convert any image into an old one. To obtain this effect, you will use two settings and two filters whose parameters need to be adapted to the photo you want to convert according to your own criteria.

1. To begin with, open the colored image you wish to convert into an old one in the Photoshop workspace. (You can also use sample image **055.jpg.**)

2. Convert the photograph into black and white. To do this, open the **Image** menu, click on the **Adjustments** command and select the **Desaturate** option.

3. Then use the **Variations** adjustment to change the color balance, contrast, and saturation of the image. Reopen the **Image** menu, click on the **Adjustments** command and select the **Variations** option.

4. At the top of the **Variations** box you can see thumbnails of the image in its original state and with the applied color variation.  As you access this setting for the first time, the two thumbnails are exactly the same. The other thumbnails are displayed in the different colors that can be applied to the

The **Variations** adjustment cannot be applied to colored photographs or pictures of 16 bits per channel.

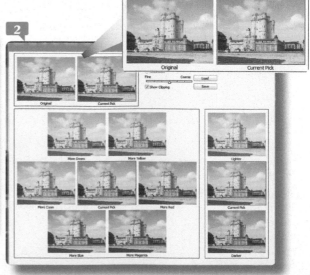

055

image. As you can see, you can apply several variations to the Shadows, Midtones (keep this option selected), Illumination and Saturation. In this example, select **More Yellow**.

5. You can see how the **Current Pick** thumbnail and the remaining ones change. Click on **More Red**.

6. Select the **Lighter** thumbnail 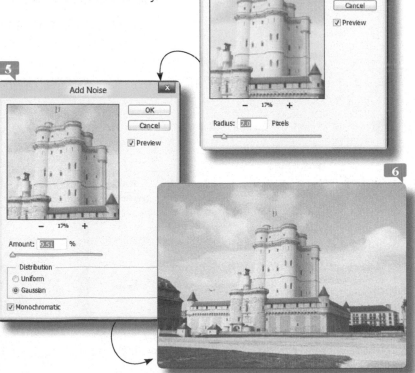 and apply the change by clicking on the **OK** button.

7. As you can see, this is another way to obtain the well-known sepia tone of old photos. To complete the effect, apply a blur and a noise filter. Open the **Filter** menu, click on the **Blur** command and select the **Gaussian Blur** option.

8. Move the slider to a value of about 2 pixels and press the **OK** button to have a look at the obtained effect.

9. Open the **Filter** menu again, click on the **Noise** command and select the **Add Noise** option.

10. Select the **Gaussian** and **Monochromatic** options and apply the percentage of noise according to the desired effect. You can get the desired effect by looking at the preview.

11. Apply the filter by clicking on the **OK** button and now you will see that the picture looks as if it was taken several years ago.

The application of the variations is **accumulative**, that is, each time you click on a thumbnail, the effect fuses the Current Pick thumbnail.

Converting a photo into a television image

IF YOU WANT A PICTURE TO LOOK LIKE it was taken from the television, you just need to follow the simple steps in this exercise. It is important that the picture you use is in RGB color mode, which you can check in the document tab.

1. To begin, open the image you would like to transform in Photoshop. (You can also use example image **056.jpg**.)

2. Press the key combination **Ctrl + N** to access the **New** box, set it at a size of **1 pixel wide** by **2 pixels high** and select a Transparent background. Click on **OK** to create the new document.

3. To display the canvas, go to the **View** menu and select the **Fit on Screen** option.

4. Select the **Pencil Tool**, which is grouped with the **Brush, Color Replacement,** and **Mixer Brush Tool** in the **Tools** panel, and choose a brush of 1 pixel in diameter from the brush selector in the Options Bar.

5. Paint on the top pixel and press the key combination **Ctrl + A** to select the entire document.

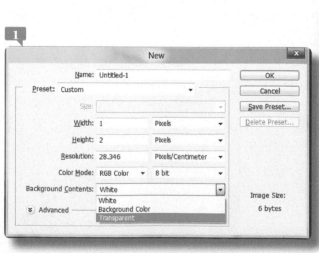

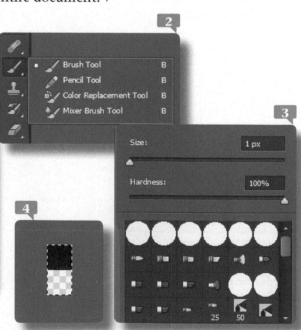

You can also open a new document in the **File** menu by clicking on the **New** option.

6. Now you need to create a pattern of this selection. Go to the **Edit** menu and click on the **Define pattern** option.

7. Apply a name to the pattern and click on the **OK** button to save it in the library.

8. Now you can close the new document without saving the changes to see the picture you want to retouch again.

9. The last step of this simple transformation is to fill the image with the pattern you just defined and with concrete values to obtain the television effect. To work more confidently, create a duplicate of the Background layer by pressing **Ctrl + J.**

10. To fill the picture, you can use the **Paint Bucket Tool** (in this case you should keep on clicking on the image to paint it by area) or the **Fill** option (which will uniformly fill the entire image). Go to the **Edit** menu and click on the **Fill** option.

11. In the **Fill** box, select the **Pattern** option in the **Use** field and in the Custom Pattern menu, locate and select the one you have created in previous steps.

12. Set an Opacity of **20%** (this value is just an orientation) and click on the **OK** button to carry out the effect.

13. Have a look at the result. If you think it is too exaggerated, you can modify the opacity of the layer by using the proper slider in the **Layers** panel.

As you create new patterns, they are added by default to the Photoshop gallery.

You can also obtain a similar result by applying a **Soft Light** blending mode with an opacity of 100%.

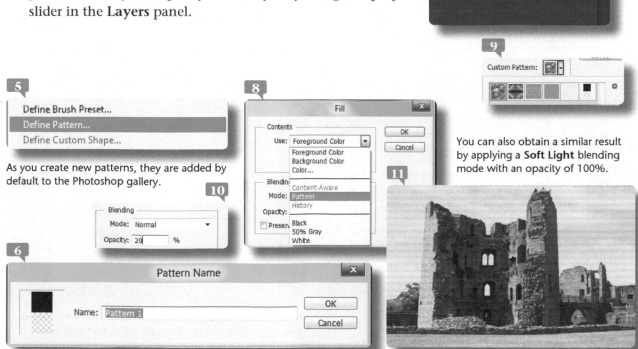

Adding text to images

TEXT IS INCLUDED IN A SINGLE LAYER and treated independently of other objects. In the Options Bar of the Type Tool you can find the options you need to set a font, change its color, increase or decrease its size, apply a kerning or tracking effect to increase or decrease the distance between the characters, scale vertically the elements of the text object or, implement minor effects such as strike through, underline, small caps, superscript, subscript, or uppercase.

1. Open any digital photograph to which you want to add text, in the workspace. (If you wish you can use sample file **057.jpg**).

2. You need to select the Text Tool and define its properties in the **Options Bar**. In the **Tools** panel, enable the **Horizontal Type** or **Vertical Type Tool** according to the orientation you want for your text.

3. As you activate the Text Tool, its configurable properties will appear in the **Options Bar**. Select a font, 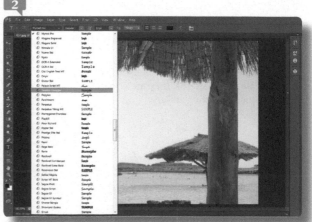 font size, and color you want to apply to your text.

4. Then click on the area of the image to which you want to add

You can also activate the **Type Tool** by pressing **T** on your keyboard.

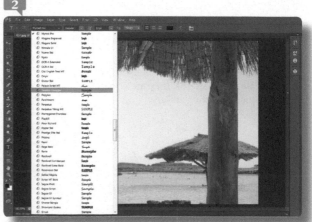

In Photoshop, the text consists of **contours of vector-based text**, which allows you to generate a text with clear edges regardless of the resolution.

the text and type your text.

5. Note that in the **Layers** panel a new layer, which only contains text, has been added. Once inserted, you can modify it by triple-clicking on the text.

6. Apply one of the distortions available in Photoshop by simply clicking on the **Create Warped Text** command, which is located to the right of the **Color** field.

7. In the **Warp Text** dialog box, display the **Style** field and select the **Flag** option.

8. Note how the style is immediately applied to the text. Open this field again and this time, select the **Fish** option.

9. You can adjust various aspects of each style provided by the program: the orientation, the percentage of curve and the horizontal and vertical distortion. To test this, drag the slider of the **Bend** field to the right and have a look at the result in the selected text.

10. Keep all other settings and apply the distortion by clicking on the **OK** button.

11. To finish the exercise, approve the changes by clicking on the last command in the **Options Bar.**

057

IMPORTANT

In Photoshop CS6, the **Character** panel includes buttons for the Open Type features such as ligatures, fractions, etc.

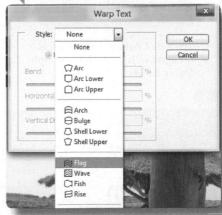

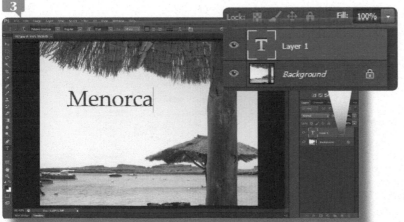

The text layers are always displayed with a thumbnail T in the **Layers** panel.

Applying character and paragraph styles

NEW CHARACTER STYLE AND PARAGRAPH STYLE panels have been added to Photoshop CS6. With the help of these tools, you can define different character and paragraph styles to apply them quickly and easily to the text of an image.

1. For this exercise, you can use sample image **057.jpg**. Open the new **Character Styles** panel in the **Window** menu.

2. The creation of a character style facilitates the implementation of a number of properties on the text, which noticeably speeds up your work. In the **Character Styles** panel, click on the third icon at the bottom called **Create new character style.**

3. This adds a new style to the panel, which is called **Character Style 1.** To access its **Options** box, double-click on that style.

4. This opens the **Character Style Options** box, where you can define the characteristics of your new style. Start by selecting a font family and then access the Color Picker to set the font color.

The new **Character Styles** panel is grouped with the new **Paragraph Styles** panel.

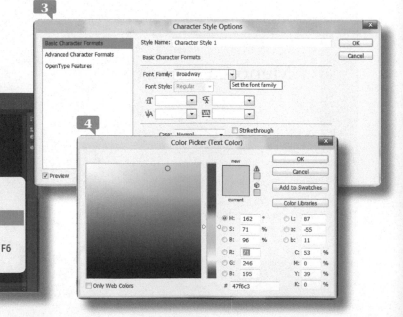

058

5. Create the new style by clicking on the **OK** button and check if the text layer, in which you are working right now and the one you created in the previous exercise, already displays the characters you just set.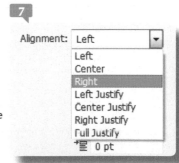

6. With the **Horizontal Type Tool**, type two lines of text on the image and access the **Paragraph Styles** panel again.

7. Create a new paragraph style by clicking on the **Create new paragraph style** icon and access its Options box by double-clicking on it.

8. In the **Paragraph Style Options** box, you can configure the basic and advanced format of the characters, the alignment options, the space, the type area of the paragraph, and so on. Enable the **Indents and Spacing** category and select, for example, **Right** alignment.

9. Create the new paragraph style by clicking on the **OK** button in its box and look at the options, which are automatically applied to the paragraph of the selected layer.

Note that you can modify the characteristics of the character and paragraph styles at any time—you just need to double-click on its Options box.

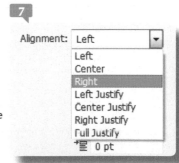

You can also retrieve the **features** of a character style in the Options Bar.

By default, Photoshop CS6 displays a character and paragraph style, to which you can add your own ones.

Creating text masks

TEXT MASKS ALLOW YOU TO add text, which then becomes a selection area that can be moved, copied, filled, and outlined like any other selection. To carry it out, Photoshop provides the Horizontal Type Mask and Vertical Type Mask Tool, which are very useful to create, for example, text with a filled image or overlay text with an image or if you want to apply any effects of shadow or lines to the mask.

1. After opening the image on which you want to create the text mask (you can use sample file **059.jpg**), click on the **Horizontal Type Tool** and select the **Horizontal Type Mask** option.

2. Click on the area of the image in which you want to insert the text.

3. Then, a red screen that covers the entire document will appear. This indicates that everything you insert from now on will be considered as a mask. Type in a sample word and select it by double-clicking on it. **1**

4. Change the font by selecting it from the font list, which is available in the **Options Bar**. **2**

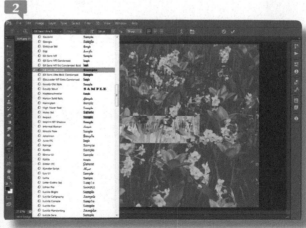

In order to obtain a striking effect, you should create a mask on an image that consists of many colors.

5. Enter the value 200 in the **Set the font size** field in the **Options Bar** [3] and click on the button **Commit any current edits**.

6. Check whether the red layer disappears and whether the added text is displayed as if it was a selection area. [4] This selection area allows you to copy and paste the occupied area to create objects with the background of the text just below the selection. Let's try it. Go to the **Edit** menu and click on the **Copy** option.

7. Press the key combination **Ctrl + N** to access the **New** box, adjust the properties of your new document, and click on **OK**.

8. Press the key combination **Ctrl + V** to paste the text mask. [5]

9. Now you need to apply an effect to the layer to highlight it. In the **Layers** panel, click on the **Options** button and select **Blending Options**.

10. In the **Layer Style** box, click on the **Stroke** option.

11. This style creates a colored outline around the selected object (have a look at it in the preview box). Click on the **Color** field. [6]

12. In the **Color Picker** box, select a new color and apply the change by clicking on the **OK** button.

13. In the **Size** field, enter the value of 5 [7] and apply the selected style by clicking on **OK**.

Imagine the quantity of spectacular labels, titles, etc., you can obtain due to the text masks and the effects provided by Photoshop. [8]

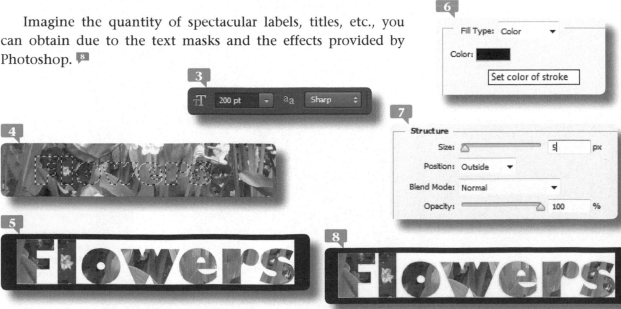

Adding text to a path

IMPORTANT

As you select the text in the path with the **Ctrl** key, you can rotate it on that path and slide it to change its location.

INSERTING TEXT INTO A PATH can be carried out by two main steps: the creation of the shape with the help of a drawing tool (such as the Pen Tool) and the insertion of the text. You can use the Freeform Pen Tool, since it allows you to draw a line that, for example, adjusts itself to the elements of a picture. Furthermore, the insertion of the text does not display any difference in reference to its normal use on a document. Once the text is inserted into the path, it can be modified in terms of size, color, or font.

1. This time, your goal is to create a freehand path that retraces the silhouette in order to, in the end, add a short text to the path. Open the image you want to work with (you can also use image **002.jpg**) and select out of the **Tools** panel the **Freeform Pen Tool**, which is grouped with the **Pen Tool** and its derivatives.

2. You need to use the drag technique to carry out the freehand path. But before doing this, you need to activate an option that facilitates the adjustment of the line to the image. Enable the **Magnetic** option in the **Options Bar**.

3. Click on the **Geometry** options icon, which is to the left of the **Magnetic** option.

In this option panel, you can define the mode of performance of the **Magnetic Pen Tool**.

060

4. In the panel that appears, you need to adjust the preferences to the path. In the **Width** field, you can assign the margin (in pixels) so you can draw with a pen in it. Further, the **Contrast** field specifies the percentage of the possible outline of the image, and the **Frequency** field controls the number of anchor points (between 5—more points—and 40—fewer points) inserted into the path. Adjust to a width of 3 pixels and enable the **Path** option in the mode selector of the tool **Options Bar.**

5. As you select the **Magnetic** option, the cursor converts to a pen with a small magnet on its right. Click on a starting point in your image, retrace the silhouette to create a path, and click on **Return** when you have finished.

6. Enable the **Horizontal Type Tool** in the **Tools** panel and click on a point of the path.

7. Before you start typing, set the font properties in the **Options Bar** (size, family, color . . .).

8. Type directly on your sample phrase and press the key combination **Ctrl + Enter** to confirm it.

9. You have just added text to a path. From here on out, you can edit the text and its aspects: size, font, alignment, style, etc. Always remember to preselect it with the **Type Tool**.

If the **Path** mode is not enabled in the Options Bar, you need to create a separate layer instead of a path.

As you adjust the text properties, you need to take into account the length of the path that it is replacing. A very large font size may mean that the text won't fit in its path.

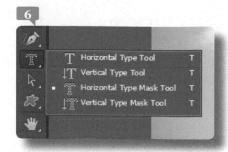

Creating a work path

YOU MIGHT NEED TO CREATE a path of a temporary shape that appears in a photograph in order to further make a selection, to copy it into another document, to fill or outline it, etc. This is a Photoshop technique that can be useful for further retouching, and in this lesson we will show you how.

1. In Photoshop, open an image that contains a shape from which you want to create a work path (you can also use sample file **002.jpg** again).

2. Enable the **Magnetic Lasso Tool**, which is grouped with the **Lasso** and **Polygonal Lasso Tool** in the **Tools** panel 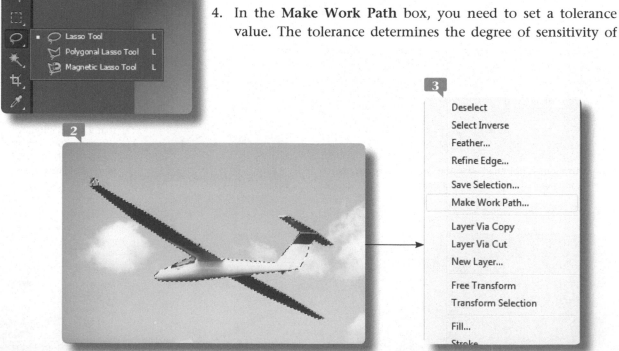 and select it by dragging the shape that you want to convert into a path. (Note that you can choose any of the selection tools to create a path from a shape.)

3. Remember that in order to create a closed selection, you need to click on the first point created with the lasso. Now click with the right mouse button on the selection and select the **Make Work Path** option out of its context menu.

4. In the **Make Work Path** box, you need to set a tolerance value. The tolerance determines the degree of sensitivity of

061

the command in reference to the changes in the shape of the selection. It can be adjusted between 0.5 and 10 pixels, and the higher the tolerance is, the fewer anchor points will be used to generate the path, which therefore implies a greater smoothness. Keep the tolerance value that appears by default and click on **OK**. 4

5. This automatically creates the path that you can modify according to your taste by adding or removing anchor points, or you can alter the points that already exist with the **Path Selection** or **Direct Selection Tool**. Click for a few seconds on the **Path Selection Tool**, which is symbolized by a white arrow, and select the **Direct Selection Tool**. 5

6. Click on various parts of the path and use the appearing dragging tool to modify its shape. 6

7. Access the **Paths** panel in the **Window** menu and check if the work path appears in there. 7

8. Fill the path with the foreground color by clicking on the button **Fill path with foreground color** (the first one in the **Paths** panel). 8 Have a look at the effect. 9

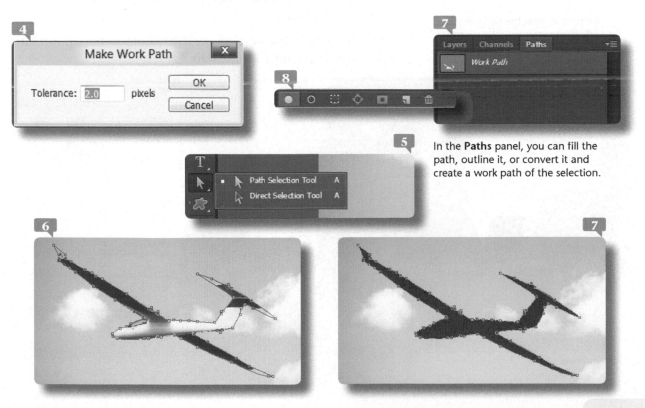

In the **Paths** panel, you can fill the path, outline it, or convert it and create a work path of the selection.

135

Converting a silhouette image to black and white

IN THIS EXERCISE WE WILL SHOW YOU a technique with which you can quickly and easily convert a color photo to a black and white photo. These pictures are very similar to the ones you can see in comics.

1. To carry out this exercise, open the image you want to transform (you can also use sample file **062.jpg**).

2. To begin the conversion, you need to remove the colors of the image without changing its color mode. Go to the **Image** menu, click on the **Adjustments** option and select **Desaturate**. **1**

3. Then, in order to add some light to the image, you need to apply an unsharp mask. Open the **Filter** menu, click on the **Sharpen** option and select the **Unsharp Mask** filter. **2**

4. Drag the three sliders of the **Unsharp Mask** box completely to the left and adjust them until you obtain the desired illumination for your image. **3**

5. Open the **Image** menu, click on the **Adjustments** option and select the **Threshold** adjustment. **4**

Remember that the **Desaturate** adjustment removes the colors of the image, but keeps its color mode.

062

6. The **Threshold** dialog box will open where you need to set the threshold level of the image. Drag the slider to obtain a sharp contrast and click on the **OK** button to apply the effect. 5

7. Apply a blur filter to the image to enhance the effect. Go to the **Filter** menu, click on the **Blur** command and select the **Gaussian Blur** option. 6

8. Note that it is better to apply a small **Gaussian blur** radius. Drag the slider until you obtain the desired effect and apply the filter by pressing the **OK** button. 7

9. In order to improve the results further, go to the **Tools** panel and select the **Eraser Tool** with a suitable brush and eliminate the spots or stains you do not like. 8

As you can see, it is an easy and effective technique. Of course, it depends on the original image and the values you apply to the different filters and established adjustments: the results can be dramatic or even more dramatic. Please feel free to practice with other images to see the differences.

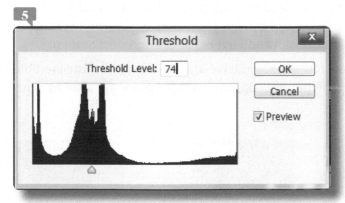

The Threshold Level is displayed as a curve at the bottom of the **Threshold** dialog box.

As you use the **Eraser Tool,** the white background of the image will appear. It allows you to remove spots, stains, and other defects resulting from the conversion and the application of the filters.

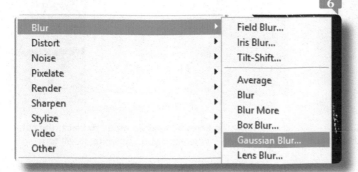

Adding fog to a photo

IN THIS EXERCISE WE WILL SHOW YOU two techniques to add a realistic fog effect to your images. In a few steps and only using the Clouds and Motion blur filters, you can create a desirable effect.

1. Open the image you want to retouch in Photoshop (you can also use sample image **063.jpg**), fit it on the screen and create a new layer by clicking on the **Create a new layer** icon in the **Layers** panel.

2. Apply the filters to this new layer. Restore black as the foreground color and white as the background color by pressing the **D** key or use the two boxes that display those colors in the **Tools** panel.

3. Go to the **Filter** menu, click on the **Render** command and select the **Clouds** option. 2

4. The filter is automatically applied to the layer and combines the background and foreground colors. Open the list of layer blending options in the **Layers** panel and select **Screen**. 3

5. With these few steps you have already created a quite credible fog effect. 4 But you can improve it by adding a slight blur.

Remember that the **Clouds** filter is directly applied without opening any configuration dialog box, and it combines the foreground and background colors.

If you apply the **Screen** blending mode to black, the color will not change, whereas if you use white, it will turn white.

Go to the **Filter** menu, click on the **Blur** command and select the **Motion Blur** option.

6. Adjust the **Distance** filter slider until you obtain the desired blur and apply it by pressing the **OK** button.

7. You can also reduce the opacity of the layer so that the fog is lighter. Now we will show you another quite similar procedure with which you can achieve the same result. Restore the original state of the image in the **History** panel.

8. Create a new layer and make sure that the foreground and background colors are white and black.

9. Enable the **Gradient Tool**, which is grouped with the **Paint Bucket** and **3D Material Drop Tool** in the **Tools** panel.

10. In the **Options Bar**, select the black to white Radial Gradient  and draw a diagonal line that goes from the top right to the bottom left.

11. Apply the **Clouds** filter to this gradient. Select it by following the menu path you already learned about.

12. Now you just need to reduce the opacity of the layer and modify it according to your taste until you obtain a realistic effect. Carry it out by using the **Opacity** slider in the **Layers** panel.

Leave the Angle field at **0°** so it is horizontal.

Adding light beams to an image

YOU CAN ADD LIGHT BEAMS TO A PHOTOGRAPH, in the same manner you insert fog, by following the steps in this exercise.

1. For this exercise, you may want to use the sample image from the previous exercise or any other outdoor photograph you have. Once opened in Photoshop, add a layer by clicking on the **Create a new layer** icon in the **Layers** panel.

2. Apply a linear black to white gradient to the new layer. Enable the **Gradient Tool**, select the appropriate options in the **Options Bar** 1 and draw the gradient by dragging it. 2

3. Go to the **Filter** menu, click on the **Render** command and select the **Difference Clouds** option. 3

4. Then you need to select the beam path. Go to the **Image** menu, click on the **Adjustments** command and select the **Levels** option.

The appearance of the gradient depends on the points on which you click as you start and finish it.

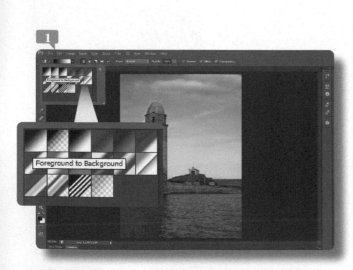

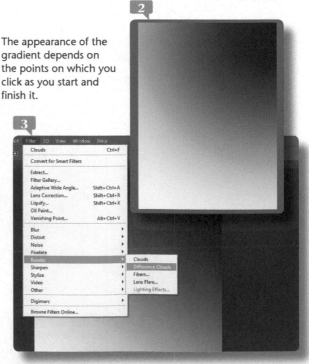

If the **Difference Clouds** filter is applied for the first time, it will produce an inversion of image fragments in the shape of a cloud. If applied repeatedly, it will result in a texture similar to marble.

5. In the **Levels** box, click on the **Auto** button 🔎 and apply the change by pressing the **OK** button.

6. Go to the **Image** menu, click on the **Adjustments** command and select the **Invert** option.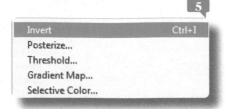

7. Now you can see what the light beam path looks like. Go back to the **Levels** box in the **Image** menu and drag the **Input Levels** sliders until you obtain a realistic look for your beam. Apply the new levels by clicking on **OK**.

8. Next, open the **Image** menu, click on the **Adjustments** command and select the **Hue/Saturation** option.

9. In order to color the light beam, select the **Colorize** option in the dialog box and choose the hue, saturation, and lighting you would like to obtain by using the corresponding sliders. 🔎

10. You can polish the beams by using the **Eraser Tool** with an appropriate brush size.

11. Select the **Screen** blending mode for this layer in the **Layers** panel and, if necessary, move the layer with the **Move Tool** until you find the right position for the beam. 🔎

064

IMPORTANT

In Photoshop CS6, all gradients now feature the **Dither** option, so they will blend better.

The gradient, which was originally in black and white, can be colored in any color chosen in the Hue control as you activate the **Colorize** option in the Hue/Saturation box.

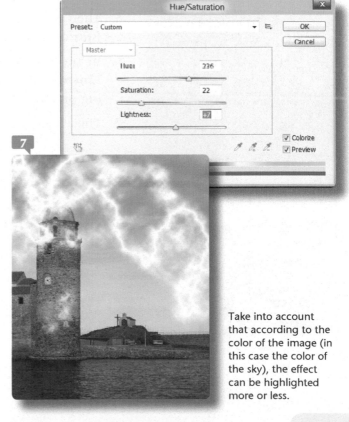

Take into account that according to the color of the image (in this case the color of the sky), the effect can be highlighted more or less.

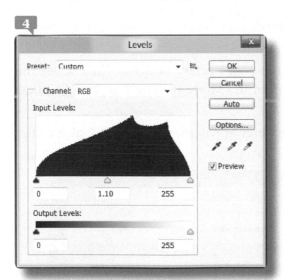

You can also access the **Levels** dialog box by pressing the key combination **Ctrl + L**.

Creating lighting effects

THERE ARE DIFFERENT TECHNIQUES with which you can add lighting effects to your images. In this exercise, you will get to know three of them, which are very simple and based on the application of the Gaussian Blur and the Diffuse Glow filter.

1. To begin, open the image you want to modify. (You can also use sample image **065.jpg**.)

2. Press the key combination **Ctrl + J** to obtain a duplicate of the **Background** layer. ▊

3. Go to the **Filter** menu, click on the **Blur** option and choose the **Gaussian Blur** filter.

4. Drag the slider in the **Radius** field up to approximately **3 pixels** (you need to set this value based on the resolution of the photograph with which you are working) and apply the filter by pressing **OK**. ▊

5. Then open the **Edit** menu and click on the **Fade Gaussian Blur** command. ▊

6. In the **Fade** box, apply an opacity of **60%**. Then select the **Linear Light** option in the **Mode** field and apply it by clicking on **OK**. ▊

7. The effect now becomes apparent. ▊ Let's look at another

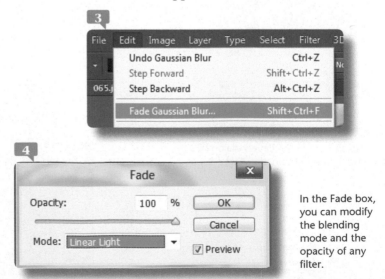

In the Fade box, you can modify the blending mode and the opacity of any filter.

142

065

process that allows you to add a lighting effect to the image. Restore the original state of the image in the **History** panel.

8. Duplicate the Background layer by pressing the key combination **Ctrl + J**.

9. Apply the **Gaussian Blur** filter again. Access the same configuration box and set a very high radius.

10. You should then reduce the opacity of the duplicate layer to obtain the desired effect. **6** Do it by using the opacity slider in the **Layers** panel. **7**

11. The third technique you are going to use here is one where you can add a lighting effect to an image.

12. Restore the initial state of the image in the **History** panel and create a duplicate of the Background layer.

13. Make sure that the foreground and background colors are black and white (you can press the D key to select them directly), go to the **Filter** menu, click on the **Distort** command and select the **Diffuse Glow** option. **8**

14. You need to modify the regulators **Graininess**, **Glow Amount**, and **Clear Amount** **9** until you have obtained the desired effect. In this example, you applied a granulate value of **5**, an amount of brightness of **5**, and an amount of clarity of **13** to obtain the brightness.

Compare the original image with the retouched ones hidden in Layer 1 to see the clear difference between them.

Adding lens flare and lighting effects

THE RENDER FILTERS ALLOW YOU to add a lighting effect to an object, such as creating spotlights and lens flares to increase and intensify the realistic representation of the images. If these spotlights are applied to a solarized image or on a Difference Clouds filter, you can truly obtain spectacular results

1. To begin, open the image you want to retouch in the Photoshop workspace. (You can also use sample file **066.jpg**.)

2. Apply the **Solarize** filter, which allows you to blend a negative image with a positive one. Create a duplicate of the Background layer by pressing the key combination **Ctrl + J** and follow the menu path **Filter/Stylize/Solarize.** 1

3. Combine this filter (you have already obtained quite spectacular results) with another one to add a flare to the image. Open the **Filter** menu, click on the **Render** option and select the **Lens Flare** filter. 2

4. The chosen filter applies a bright area simulating the refraction of a camera. By default, the flash appears in the center of the image and with a percentage of 100%. Select the lens type **105mm Prime**, set a percentage of 135% brightness and move the flare of the preview by dragging it to the desired location

The **Solarize** filter is directly applied and has no configurable parameters.

1

2

in your image  (of course, you can use other values if the result doesn't satisfy you).

5. Apply the filter by pressing the **OK** button and have a look at the beautiful effect.  Now you need to apply a lighting effect to the Difference Clouds filter, which is another way to obtain the same effect. Access the **History** panel and restore the status of the image before the **Solarize** filter was applied.

6. Select a dark red as a foreground color and choose white as the background color.

7. Open the **Filter** menu, click on the **Render** command and select this time the **Difference Clouds** option.

8. Although the result is pretty spectacular, it can be improved by applying a lighting effect to the image. Open the **Filter** menu again, click on the **Render** command and select the **Lighting Effects** option.

9. New to Photoshop CS6 is that the Properties panel of the Lighting Effects box opens, where you can adjust the properties according to your preferences.  Other configuration options are located in the Options Bar. Go to the **Presets** field and select, for example, the **Crossing down** style.

10. Change the intensity and location of the flare by adjusting it with the help of the controls in the workspace.  Choose another color for the light in the parameters panel and apply the effect.

Have a look at the difference between the application of a lighting effect or of a flash to your images.

In Photoshop CS6, the application of the lighting effects is more interactive and can be carried out from the workspace.

Giving relief to a photo

THERE ARE DIFFERENT TECHNIQUES to give relief to an image. Some of them require, or at least suggest, the conversion to grayscale if the photography is in color. In this exercise we will focus on the usage of two filters: the Bas Relief and the Emboss filter, which can be found in different options of the Filter menu.

1. Open the image you want to retouch in Photoshop. You can use your own picture or choose one of the sample files.

2. To begin, you need to create a duplicate layer so that the original image is always available in the **Background** layer. Press the key combination **Ctrl + J** to carry this out.

3. The first change you need to perform is to convert the image to grayscale. Go to the **Image** menu, click on the **Mode** option and select **Grayscale**.

4. Then, Photoshop will ask you if you want to flatten the layers as you realize the change. To keep the Background layer intact, click on the **Don't Flatten** button. **2**

5. In the next dialog box, click on the **Discard** button to discard the color information. **3** Now the image is in grayscale.

6. Now you need to invert the colors. Go to the **Image** menu, click on the **Adjustments** command and select the **Invert** option.

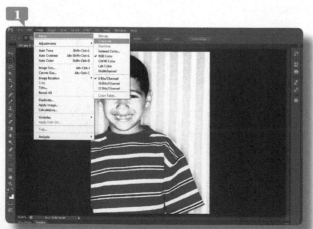

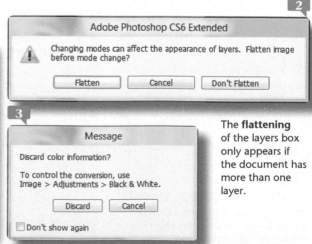

The **flattening** of the layers box only appears if the document has more than one layer.

067

7. You have now obtained some kind of negative of the photograph. 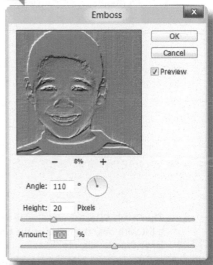 Open the **Filter** menu, click on the **Sketch** command and select the **Bas Relief** filter.

8. Now you need to adjust the **Detail**, **Smoothness**, and **Light** parameters of this filter to obtain a result you like. You can also use the preview on the left. If you use example image **067.jpg**, enter the value **12** in the **Detail** field, the value **10** in the **Smoothness** field, and maintain the light as **Bottom**.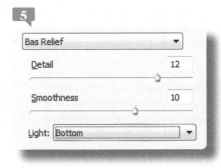

9. Have a look at the result.  You can also obtain a relief effect if you use the **Emboss** filter in the **Stylize** category. Restore the **Layer via Copy** condition of the photograph in the **History** panel.

10. Open the **Filter** menu, click on the **Stylize** command and select the **Emboss** filter.

11. Modify the filter settings until you obtain the desired result, which, among other things, will depend on the resolution of the image. As an example, set at an angle of **110°**, a height of **20 pixels**, and an Amount of **100%** and apply the filter.

12. The result is already striking, but you could change the filter transition mode in order to give the image more dimensions without modifying its colors. Open the **Edit** menu and click on the **Fade Emboss** option.

13. Select and apply the **Darker Color** blending mode and have a look at the difference between the original and the retouched photo, which is hidden and displayed in **Layer 1**.

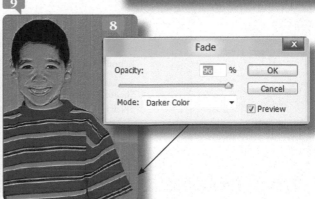

Modifying images with brushes

BRUSHES ARE USED TO MODIFY AN IMAGE by giving it a particular style. You can change the predetermined characteristics of the brushes or you can create your own brush type. Photoshop also displays the Brush panel, which allows you to change the shape, content, and size of any brush. Further, you can save the new brush, so you can use it again as you need it.

1. To begin, open the photo you want to retouch (you can also use sample file **068.jpg**) and click on the **Create a new layer** option in the **Layers** panel.

2. Then click on the **Brush Tool** in the Tools panel.

3. In the **Options Bar**, click on the brush selector arrow and click on the **Options** button on the right to enter the menu with the different brush types.

4. Select **Special Effect Brushes**. **1**

5. In the warning box about replacing the brushes group, just click on **OK** to confirm. **2**

6. In the Brushes box, select the brush type with the number **29**. **3**

7. In the **Options Bar**, double-click on the **Opacity** field, enter the value **80** and press **Enter**.

The **Brush Selector** can display them in different ways: a list with only the name of the brush, with small or large thumbnails, etc.

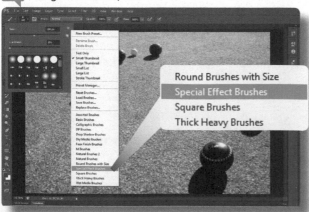

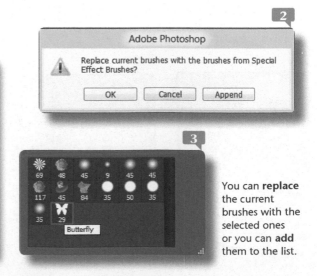

You can **replace** the current brushes with the selected ones or you can **add** them to the list.

068

8. As you can see, the selected brush applies a different color and size to each butterfly, and increases the authenticity of the applied element. Click on the different parts of your image and have a look at the result.

9. We do not want to end this exercise without you using the **Mixer Brush Tool**, which was new in Photoshop CS5 and which can simulate real painting techniques. Open example image **041.jpg**. Find the **Mixer Brush Tool**, which is grouped with the **Brush Tool**, and select it.

10. Now you need to apply a color you like to the brush. You can select a default foreground color or any other color of the canvas. To do this, press the **Alt** key and without releasing it, click on the flower.

11. In the **Options Bar**, you can configure the tool. Within these options, there are a few interesting parameters: the **Wet** parameter, which controls how much paint the brush picks up from the canvas, the **Load** parameter, which specifies the amount of paint loaded in the reservoir, and the **Mix** parameter, which controls the ratio of canvas paint to reservoir paint. It also has a brush style selector with predetermined characteristics. We recommend practicing on your own by adjusting these parameters until you obtain the strokes you need. In this example, select the **Moist** style and paint on the petals.

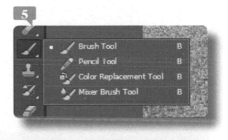

The brush can be applied by keystrokes or by dragging. The program also allows you to create straight lines by holding down the **Shift** key.

Creating a burnt edge effect

THIS EXERCISE WILL SHOW you a simple technique for adding a burnt edge effect to a photograph. As always, the values displayed in this exercise are approximate, and you need to adjust them to the image you are working with.

1. Open the image to which you want to add edges (you can also use example image **069.jpg**) and duplicate the Background layer by pressing the key combination **Ctrl + J**.

2. Enable the **Lasso Tool** and, by dragging, draw an irregular selection as a framework for the image with a Fade value of 0 pixels on the duplicated layer.

3. Open the **Select** menu, click on the **Modify** command and select the **Feather** option.

4. As a function of depth, set the desired Feather Radius for the selection, and then invert it by selecting the menu path **Select/Inverse**.

5. The next step is to create a new channel with this edge selection. Open the **Select** menu, click on the **Save Selection** option and enter a descriptive name in the box and click on **OK**.

When you save your selection with the Lasso Tool, choose a descriptive name that you can easily remember since you will need to reload it later.

069

6. Go to the **Channels** panel and see how the new channel has been added.  Then press the **Delete** key to delete the part of the selected image in both layers and invert the selection by pressing the key combination **Shift + Ctrl + I**.

7. Now you have selected the image and not the edge path with the Lasso. Then, with the help of the **Eyedropper Tool**, you need to take a sample of the color of the image that will be applied to the edge.

8. Select the **Background** layer and load the selection you have saved before you followed the route **Select/Load Selection** and apply to it a Fade of approximately 10 pixels.

9. Open the **Edit** menu, click on the **Fill** option and fill the selection with the chosen foreground color in the **Hard Light** blending mode.

10. Reload the selection of the edge, apply a Fade of approximately 6 pixels and fill the selection with the foreground color. But this time, enable the **Multiply** blending mode. (To carry this out, just repeat the previous two steps.)

11. Press the key combination **Ctrl + D** to deselect the edge and have a look at the first result. To finish the exercise, hide the background layer by clicking on its Visibility icon to see the final effect on a transparent background.

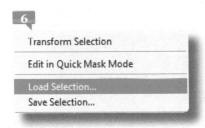

You can load a saved selection in another image, but you need to open the original image and the target image.

Creating a ghost effect

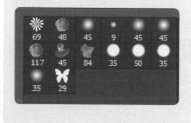
WITH THE HELP OF THIS EXERCISE YOU can transform the image of a person into a terrifying ghost and place it on any background.

1. Open the picture on which you want to apply the ghost effect (you can use the sample image **070.jpg**) and use the **Extract** filter (see exercise 37) to remove the person from the background. 🗨

2. Now the person is displayed on a transparent background. Open the **Image** menu, click on the **Adjustments** option and select **Black & White**. 🗨

3. To achieve the first ghost effect, adjust the **Black & White** box until you obtain your desired result. You should set the Yellow controller to a very high value and apply a greenish nuance with a low Saturation to improve the effect. 🗨

4. Then enable the **Smudge Tool** in the **Tools** panel, 🗨 select a medium soft brush, adjust the Opacity to about 80%, and go up by clicking and dragging the button of the photo to blur this area.

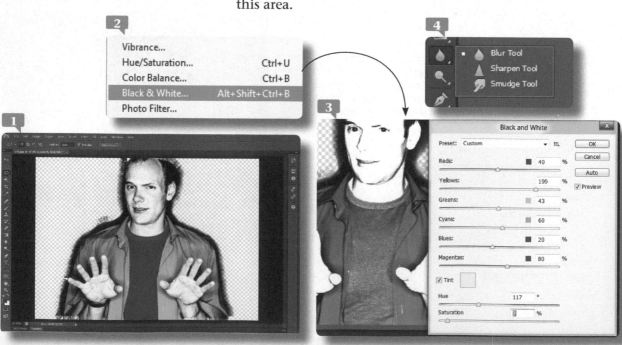

5. Press the key combination **Ctrl + J** to duplicate the layer, open the **Filter** menu, click on the **Blur** option and select the **Gaussian Blur** filter.

6. Set a Radius of about 5 pixels, apply the Blur and select the **Lighten** blending mode for this layer in the **Layers** panel. 5

7. Create a duplicate of this layer by pressing the key combination the **Ctrl + J**, also apply the **Gaussian Blur**, but this time adjust the Radius about twice as much as before and select the **Lighten** blending mode again.

8. Now select the first layer in the **Layers** panel, open the **Filter** menu, click on the **Blur** command and select this time the **Motion Blur** option.

9. Set an approximate Angle of **60°** and a Distance of about **10 pixels** and apply the Blur. 6

10. Press the **Options** button in the **Layers** panel, click on the **Blending Options** command and select the **Outer Glow** option 7 in the **Layer Style** box.

11. Define the properties of the Outer Glow effect until you achieve the desired result. Choose an appropriate color for the background where you want to place the image. 8

12. Now you just need to complete the glow effect by retouching it with the **Smudge Tool**. Select the **Scattered Dry** brush and click and drag with it on the outside of the person until you obtain the desired effect. 9

Creating a drawing effect

THERE ARE DIFFERENT FILTERS IN PHOTOSHOP that allow you to convert a photograph into an image that seems to be drawn (with a pencil, watercolors, a brush, etc.). The Sketch filters are used especially for adding a specific texture to an image, which occasionally results in an image that appears hand-drawn.

1. Open the image you want to work with in Photoshop (you can also use sample file **071.jpg**) and create a duplicate of the Background layer by pressing the key combination **Ctrl + J**.

2. The first method to obtain a drawing effect is based on the application of the **Poster Edges** filter. Open the **Filter** menu, click on the **Artistic** option and select this filter.

3. Now you need to define the desired values of the Edge Thickness, Edge Intensity, and Posterization of the filter. If you use our sample image, select an Edge Thickness of **5**, an Edge Intensity of **3**, and a Posterization of **0** and apply the filter.

4. To enhance the effect, open the **Filter** menu, click on the **Stylize** command and select the **Diffuse** filter.

5. In the **Diffuse** box, enable the **Anisotropic** option, apply the filter and see how the image is affected.

In order to examine the filter effect better before you apply it, adjust the image in the preview by using the **Fit in View** option.

071

6. Now you need to use a Sketch filter to create a buffer effect. Restore the **Layer Via Copy** state in the **History** panel and close the tab group.

7. The **Stamp** filter is applied to the selected foreground and background colors in the **Tools** panel. Change the two colors to dark green and yellow, for example.

8. Open the **Filter** menu, click on the **Sketch** command and select the **Stamp** option. **6**

9. The configurable parameters of this filter are **Light/Dark Balance** and **Smoothness**. Modify them to achieve your desired result and apply the filter. **7**

10. You can complete the effect by adding a slight **Gaussian Blur** to the layer in order to smooth the points.

11. There is also another method. With the help of this technique, you can convert the photo into a painting drawn by a brush. This time you need to use a filter of an artistic nature. Again, restore the **Layer Via Copy** state in the **History** panel. **8**

12. Open the **Filter** menu, click on the **Artistic** command and select the **Paint Daubs** option. **9**

13. The effect is immediately applied, as you see it in the preview of the Filter options box. Modify the **Brush Size** and **Sharpness** sliders and after you have tried out the effect for the different available brush types, select the one you like and apply the filter. **10**

The **Stamp** filter applies the selected background and foreground colors.

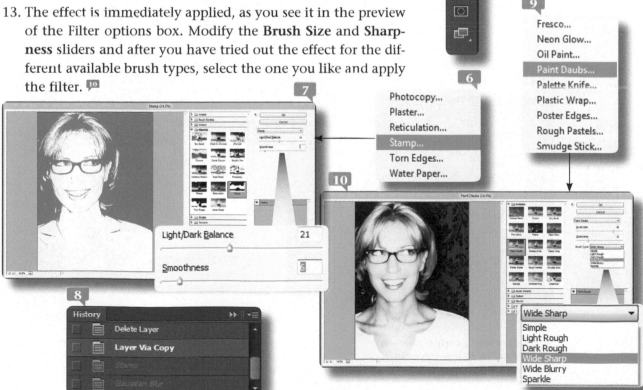

155

Creating a photocopy effect

THERE IS ANOTHER FILTER INCLUDED in the Sketch option, which allows you to get a photograph that looks like a photocopy, by following just a few steps.

1. For this exercise, you can use sample image **072.jpg**, which can be found in the download area of our website. Since we want to get the effect of a black and white photocopy, you need to select these two colors as background and foreground colors. Click on the icon of the two boxes in the **Tools** panel that represent the background and foreground colors. (You can also restore the default background and foreground colors by pressing the **D** key on your keyboard.) **1**

2. Make a duplicate of the Background layer by pressing the key combination the **Ctrl + J**. **2**

3. Remember that this mode always displays the original state of your image in the **Background** layer. Select the duplicated layer, open the **Filter** menu, click on the **Sketch** command and select the **Photocopy** option. **3**

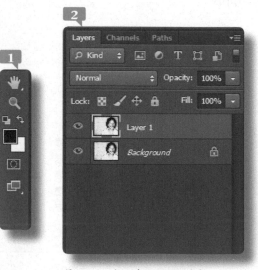

If you work with a **copy** of the Background layer, you can easily recover the original image at any time.

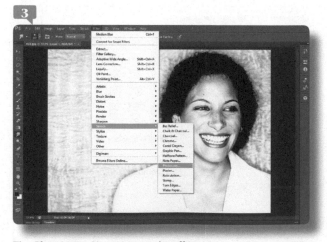

The **Photocopy** filter imitates the effect of photocopying an image. Large areas of darkness tend to copy themselves only around their edges, and the midtones, such as black or white, remain solid.

072

4. If you cannot see the entire image in the preview box, select the **Fit in View** option in the Zoom menu. 4

5. Now you can see that this simple filter has two parameters, called **Detail** and **Darkness**, which allow you to obtain a dirtier or cleaner image. Increase the Detail level, set the Darkness to about a half 5 and apply the filter.

6. The effect has been accomplished! 6 To add some color to the photocopy, open the layer blending mode options and select **Lighten**. 7

7. Try out the different layer blending options to discover the effects that can be achieved 8 and then restore the **Normal** mode.

8. To finish this exercise, modify the Output Levels of the image to obtain a clear photocopy effect. Open the **Image** menu, click on the **Adjustments** command and select the **Levels** option.

9. Drag the black slider of the output levels to the right 9 and see how the black tones of the image brighten up.

10. Apply the change by pressing the **OK** button to finish this exercise.

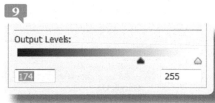

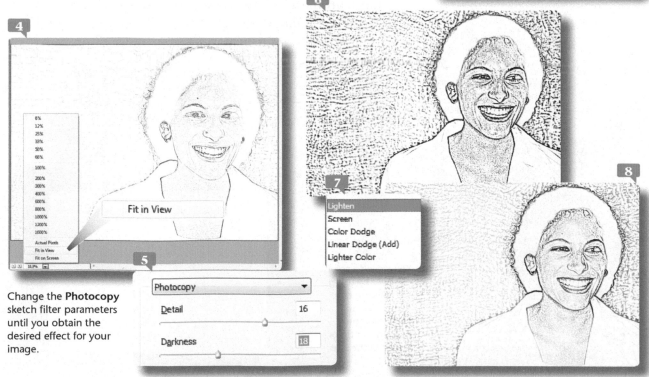

Change the **Photocopy** sketch filter parameters until you obtain the desired effect for your image.

Adding rain to a photo

THERE ARE DIFFERENT TECHNIQUES WITH WHICH you can add a rain effect to a photo. In this exercise you will get to know one of them. It is based on a combination of the Add Noise and Motion blur filter.

1. To begin, open the photo you want to retouch in Photoshop. The picture you want to work with should preferably contain a landscape on a cloudy day. You can also use sample image **073.jpg**.

2. Click on the **Create a new layer** icon in the **Layers** panel.

3. Now you need to fill the new layer with white. Select this color as the foreground color, enable the **Paint Bucket Tool** and click on **Layer 1** to color it completely.

4. Open the **Filter** menu, click on the **Noise** command and select the **Add Noise** filter.

5. Drag the **Amount** slider to **75%**, keep the **Gaussian** and **Monochromatic** options selected and apply the filter. Of course, the amount you select depends on your picture and the effect you want to achieve.

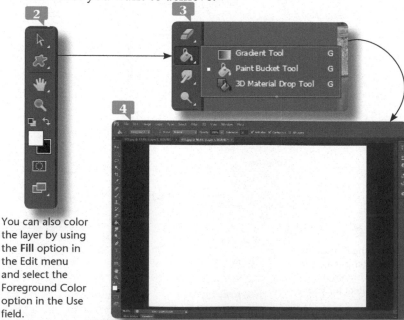

You can obtain a very similar result to this exercise if you fill the new layer with **black**.

You can also color the layer by using the **Fill** option in the Edit menu and select the Foreground Color option in the Use field.

073

6. Apply a motion blur on this filter in order to tilt the raindrops. Open the **Filter** menu, click on the **Blur** command and select the **Motion Blur** option.

7. Depending on the effect you want to achieve, you need to assign different degrees of inclination. For example, if you want to obtain a stormy effect with a lot of wind, set the degree of inclination to about 30 degrees. In this example, enter the value of **75** in the **Angle** field.

8. In the **Distance** field for example, enter the value of **35** and apply the filter by pressing **OK**. 🔲

9. If you wish, you can add a slight **Gaussian Blur** to obtain a more realistic effect.

10. Now you just need to apply the adequate blending mode to the layer. Try out **Lighten** or **Screen**, 🔲 and if the rain is too dense, you can reduce the opacity of the layer and adjust the Opacity slider to achieve the desired effect. 🔲

11. You can also modify the sliders of the Adjustment panel to brighten or darken the picture and to obtain different rain effects.

This step defines the length of the line of the water drops and its angle of fall.

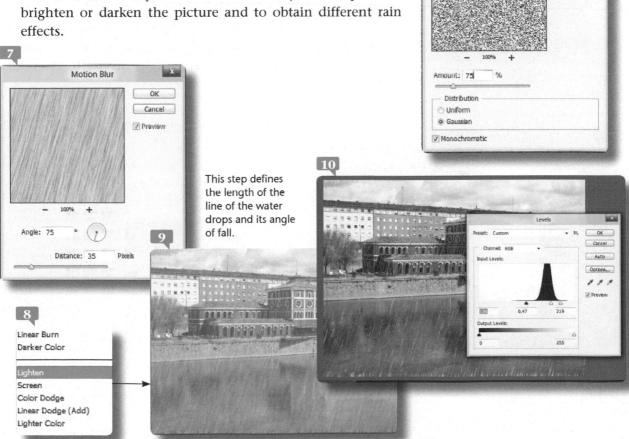

Applying a plastic effect

THE ARTISTIC PLASTIC FILTER WRAP covers an image with glossy plastic, which highlights the detail of its surface. In general, filters are used to achieve artistic painting effects for commercial projects or fine arts, but you can also obtain certain textures by using some sketch filters such as the Chrome filter.

1. For this exercise, you should use any picture stored on your computer or sample picture **074.jpg**. Once you have opened the image in Photoshop, duplicate its Background layer by pressing the key combination **Ctrl + J**.

2. Select the duplicated layer, open the **Filter** menu, click on the **Artistic** command and select the **Plastic Wrap** option. 🔲

3. In the filter box, paste the image into the preview window by using the **Fit in View** option in the Zoom menu. 🔲

4. You can determine the Highlight Detail, Strength, and Smoothness of the Plastic Wrap effect. If you work with the sample image, increase the **Highlight Strength** slider to a value of **16**.

If you are unsure to which category a filter belongs, you can access the **Filter Gallery** in the **Filter** menu where you will find it.

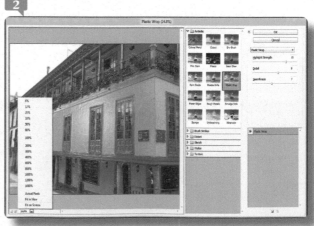

If you fit the image in the preview window of the Filter options box, you can have a better look at the effect.

5. Modify the detail of the effect by dragging the **Detail** slider to the left until it is set to **5**.

6. Drag the **Smoothness** slider until you obtain a value of **15** to smoothen the plastic effect.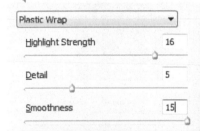

7. Apply the filter by pressing the **OK** button and have a look at the obtained effect.

8. Restore the **Layer Via Copy** state in the **History** panel and close the tab group.

9. You can see that it is also possible to obtain a plastic-like texture as you use the **Chrome** sketch filter. Locate the filter in the menu and select it.

10. Paste your picture into the Preview again and move the **Detail** and **Smoothness** sliders to obtain the desired effect.

11. As you can see, this filter converts the image to black and white, and gives it a glassy and metallic look without further modifications. The plastic texture is achieved by changing the blending mode of the layer. Select the **Lighten** blending mode and see how the chrome effect blends with the original layer to obtain a great result.

074

Modify the parameters of the **Plastic Wrap** filter according to the intensity of the desired effect.

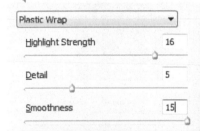

In order to add color to an image to which you want to apply the **Chrome** filter, you can reduce the opacity of the layer with the filter or you can change the layer blending mode.

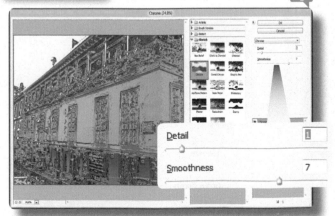

Creating a mosaic effect

AS THE PLASTIC EFFECT can be obtained in several ways, it is also possible to transform a picture into a mosaic by using two filters, which are included in the Texture category. With this exercise, you will find it very quick and easy.

1. To begin the exercise, open the image to which you want to apply a mosaic effect in Photoshop or use sample image **075.jpg** and, as always, create a duplicate of the Background layer by pressing the key combination **Ctrl + J**.

2. Open the **Filter** menu, click on the **Texture** option and select the **Mosaic Tiles** filter.

3. Fit the picture in the preview of the Filter options box.

4. It is possible to adjust the tile size (with which you want to create the mosaic), the grout width (which is the space between the tiles), and the lighten grout option. In order to increase the tile size, drag the **Tile Size** slider to the right.

5. Then, decrease the Grout Width by dragging the corresponding slider to the left.

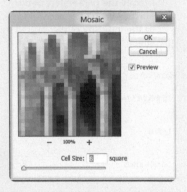

The texture filters are usually used in images to obtain an appearance of depth, substance, or to add a more natural look.

075

6. Note that if the Grout Width is very small, you will not notice the effect of the modification of the Lighten Grout parameter. To make the gap between the tiles as dark as possible, drag the **Lighten Grout** slider to the left.

7. Apply the filter and have a look at the result. You can soften the mosaic tile effect by reducing the Opacity of the layer where you applied the filter by half.

8. Recall the **Layer Via Copy** state in the **History** panel.

9. Display the **Filter** menu again, click on the **Texture** command and this time select the **Patchwork** filter.

10. This filter is perhaps the best option to achieve a mosaic effect. Fit the picture in the preview window.

11. In this case, you can change the size of the squares of the mosaic and the quantity of the relief. Increase the square size by dragging the **Square Size** slider to **10**.

12. Set the **Relief** to **15** by dragging the appropriate slider and apply the filter by pressing the **OK** button.

IMPORTANT

You can also obtain a nice mosaic effect by using the **Stained Glass** texture filter and modifying its parameters.

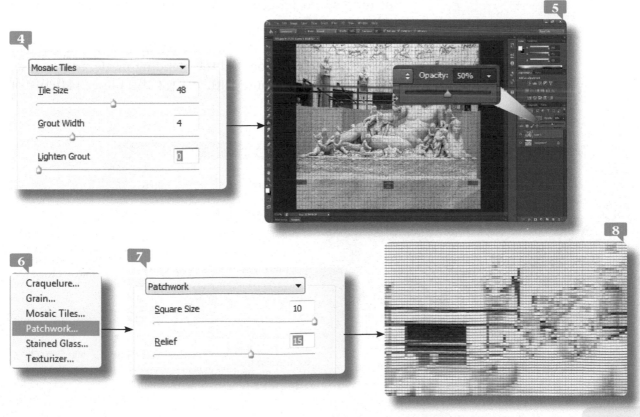

Creating picture frames

IMPORTANT

You can also obtain great frames for your photos by applying different **Filters** to the selection that has been filled.

THERE ARE TWO EASY WAYS TO CREATE picture frames. The first one is to use the Fill option in the Edit menu and the second one is the application of the Stroke style layer. In both cases, Photoshop allows you to choose the color you want to apply to the frame: it can be a single color, gradient, a motif, etc.

1. To begin this exercise, open the photo that you want to add a frame to in the Photoshop worspace and create a duplicate of your Background layer by pressing the key combination **Ctrl + J.**

2. With the **Lasso Tool**, draw a closed irregular shape around the image. You can select the tool in the **Tools** panel, and create the irregular selection by dragging it. 🔲1

3. Open the **Select** menu and click on the **Inverse** option. 🔲2

4. Thus, the part of the image that has been selected is going to be turned into a frame. Open the **Edit** menu and click on the **Fill** option. 🔲3

5. In the **Fill** box, you need to choose the color you want to use to fill the selection and the blending mode. In this case, you will create a frame with one of the preset patterns of

Remember that in order to **close a trace** realized with the Lasso Tool, you should click on the first point of it.

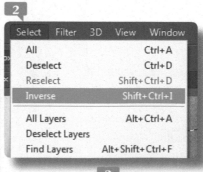

You can also invert a selection by pressing the key combination **Shift + Ctrl. + I.**

You can also access the Fill box by pressing the key combination **Shift + F5.**

Photoshop. Open the menu of the **Use** field and select the **Pattern** option. [4]

6. Now click on the cursor button in the **Custom** pattern field and select one of the choices listed in the table. [5]

7. Keep the other options as they appear in this table, press the **OK** button to see the achieved effect [6] and deselect the frame by pressing the key combination **Ctrl + D**.

8. As you can see, the first method is quite simple and fast. Now you will carry out the second technique. Restore the History status **Layer Via Copy**, open the options menu in the **Layers** panel and click on the **Blending Options** command.

9. In the **Layer Style** box, select the **Stroke** option of the left panel. [7]

10. So that the trace is created on the inside of the picture, select the **Inside** option in the **Position** field. [8]

11. Drag the **Size** slider until your frame displays the desired width. (You can see the result in the image.)

12. Now you need to apply a gradient to the frame. Open the **Fill Type** fields and select **Gradient**. [9]

13. In the Gradient box, select the one you like and apply the style.

14. Press the **OK** button to apply the style and have a look at the fantastic frame that was created for your image. [10]

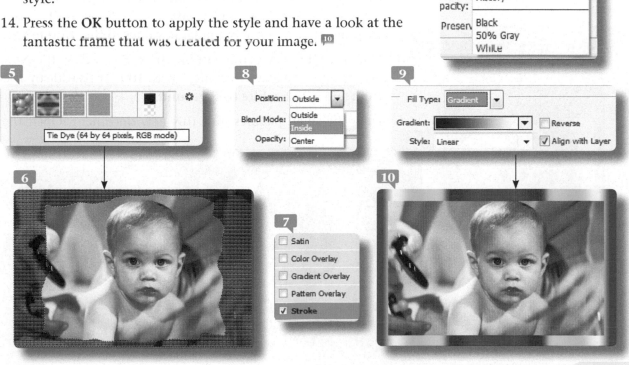

Filling an image with other images

THE MAIN STEP TO FILL A PHOTO with other images is to create a pattern with the mosaic of images with which we will fill the main image. Once you have created this pattern, in order to obtain better results, you simply need to fill the picture with it and apply it to the Layer blending mode.

1. To begin, open the images you want to work with in Photoshop. Note that you need a main image (which you are going to fill) and two (or more) images, which are going to serve as fillers. If you'd like to, you can use sample images **077-001.jpg**, **077-002.jpg**, and **077-003.jpg**.

2. Enable the **Crop Tool** and set a fixed width and height of **1500 pixels** in the **Options Bar**. 🔳 Then double-click on the crop square that appears on the image 🔳 so you can crop it.

3. Press the key combination **Ctrl + 0** to fit the image to the screen. 🔳

4. Then you need to crop sidewise a square of **50 pixels** on the images that will serve as filler. Select the second image, type these values into the **Options Bar** of the **Crop Tool** 🔳 and crop the image. 🔳 Apply the same values to the third image.

5. Now press the key combination **Ctrl + N** to access the **New** box and create a blank document with **100 pixels** wide by **100 high** and with a **white background**.

6. Drag the small pictures into this new document. Open the

It is recommended that the main image is large and has enough resolution to produce a better result.

077

Window menu, click on the **Arrange** command and select the **Tile All Vertically** option.

7. With the help of the **Move Tool**, drag one of the small images to the upper left corner of the new blank document and drag the other one to the opposite corner.

8. As you add images, layers are created. Press the key combination **Ctrl + J** to duplicate the last layer, and also duplicate **Layer 1**. Then, by dragging, place the four images in this way, so that the document is completely filled 🔲 and attach the image by using the appropriate option in the **Options** menu of the **Layers** panel.

9. After creating the mosaic (you can close the two small images without saving the changes), open the **Edit** menu, select the **Define Pattern** option and choose a name for the pattern. 🔲

10. Open the **Window** menu, click on the **Arrange** command and select the **Consolidate All to Tabs** option.

11. Select the main image, create a new layer by clicking on the **Create new layer** icon in the **Layers** panel, open the **Edit** menu and select the **Fill** option.

12. Select the **Pattern** option in the **Use** field, locate and select with a double-click the customized pattern (the one you have just created) 🔲 and apply the fill.

13. Now you either need to modify the opacity of the layer or adjust the blending modes until you obtain the best result. Apply the **Soft Light** blending mode, reduce the opacity of the layer and have a look at the beautiful effect. 🔲

You can create patterns with more than two images and with different sizes. Further, you can **desaturate** the mosaic to get the pattern in black and white, which makes it look a bit more sophisticated.

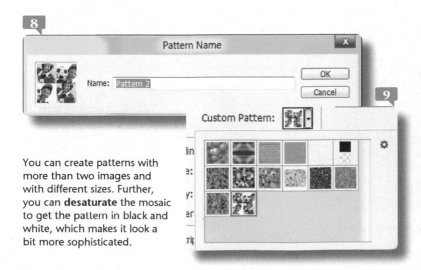

Repairing an old photo

IT IS ALMOST CERTAIN THAT YOU HAVE many old and badly damaged pictures in your photo box, which you would like to restore. With the Clone Stamp Tool and Healing Brush Tool, and with lot of patience, you can carry out most of the corrections to repair cracks, stains, etc. Then, you can complete the restoration with the necessary filters to improve them, and you can adjust the hue, brightness, and saturation.

1. To begin, open the damaged picture you want to restore in Photoshop or use sample file **078.jpg**. Create a duplicate of the **Background** layer by pressing the key combination **Ctrl + J**.

2. You need to start to fix the bottom of the image. Select the **Clone Stamp Tool** in the **Tools** panel, 🔲 set the brush properties appropriate to the area you want to retouch 🔲 and take a first sample from a spot close to the one you want to fix. Remember to press the **Alt** key while you are clicking on it.

3. Correct the entire bottom of the image like that. (Adjust the size and the hardness of the brush according to the areas you want to retouch.) 🔲

4. Once the background is fixed, select the **Healing Brush Tool** in the **Tools** panel. 🔲

You can also activate the **Clone Stamp Tool** by pressing the **S** key on your keyboard.

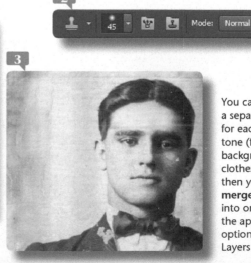

You can create a separate layer for each editing tone (face, background, clothes, etc.) and then you can **merge** them all into one by using the appropriate option in the Layers panel.

078

5. Remember that this tool works like the Clone Stamp, with the difference that it adjusts the cloning with the lighting and the tone of the sample. Continue to correct the damaged areas of your photo (if you are working with the sample image, fix the face, sleeves, and lapel of the jacket). Remember: you need to adjust the brush and take samples of the spots that are the closest to the ones you want to fix and which do not contain any imperfections. (You can increase the display zoom to work more in detail.) 5

6. Once you have fixed all cracks, stains, wrinkles, etc., you can continue to edit the image in terms of color, brightness, tone, effects, etc. Duplicate Layer 1 by pressing the key combination **Ctrl + J.**

7. In this example, you need to apply a levels adjustment layer with one of the preset values to brighten the areas with shadow. Click on the second icon in the **Create** panel, which corresponds to the **Levels** option. 6

8. You can see how an adjustment layer is automatically added on the last layer. Open the menu of preset levels in the **Properties** panel and select the **Midtones Brighter** option. 7

9. Of course, you should adjust the levels (and all the other properties of the image) according to the photograph you are working with. To finish, open the History panel in the **Window** menu and compare your original photo 8 with the one you have obtained after the last retouch. 9

7

Default

Darker
Increase Contrast 1
Increase Contrast 2
Increase Contrast 3
Lighten Shadows
Lighter
Midtones Brighter
Midtones Darker

Custom

8

5

4

Spot Healing Brush Tool   J
Healing Brush Tool   J
Patch Tool   J
Remix Tool
Red Eye Tool   J

6

Adjustments   Styles
Levels

9

Adding a crack effect to a photograph

THE TEXTURIZER FILTER, WHICH IS INCLUDED in the Texture category, allows you to add different textures to a photograph. The default textures offered by this filter are Brick, Burlap, Canvas, and Sandstone, but you can increase this number by adding new textures that you have saved on your computer in the Photoshop format. In this exercise, you will use this filter to create a cracking effect on a photograph.

1. For this exercise, you need two files: one of the image you want to retouch and one of the texture you want to apply to it. You can use sample texture **079.psd**. Open the main image and create a duplicate of the Background layer by pressing the key combination **Ctrl + J**.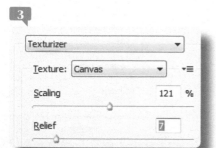

2. Open the **Filter** menu, click on the **Texture** category and select the **Texturizer** filter.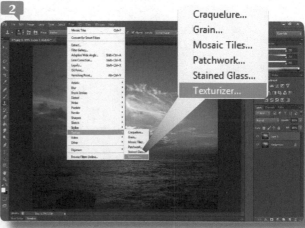

3. Fit the photo in the preview.

4. Before you load the crack texture you want to apply to the picture, have a look at the default textures offered in Photoshop. Modify the **Scaling** and **Relief** sliders of the **Canvas** texture  so that the image looks like it was painted on a canvas.

5. See the effect you obtain if you apply the other available tex-

Some filters, such as **Texturizer**, allow you to load and use other images, such as textures and displacement maps, to create the effects.

079

tures: **Brick**, **Burlap,** and **Sandstone** 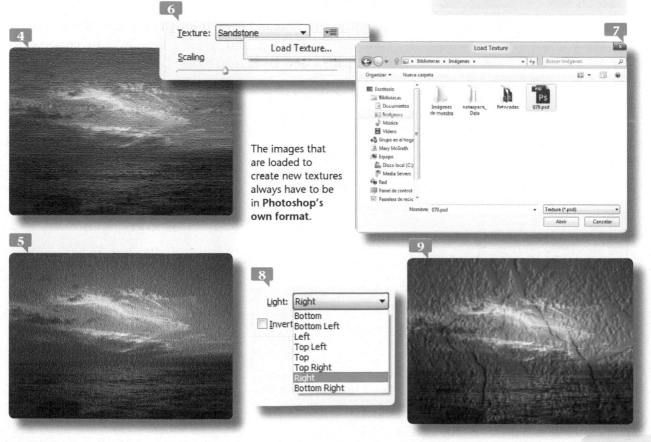 with different scales and reliefs.

6. Now you need to load the texture you want to use to crack the picture. Click on the icon to the right of the texture and click on **Load Texture.**

7. In the **Load Texture** box, locate and select the Photoshop file, which contains the texture, and open it by clicking on the **Open** button.

8. The effect will be more or less obvious depending on the size of the texture document and the image that is duplicated in the entire photo. Increase the filter scale by dragging the **Scale** slider to the right and increase in the exact manner the relief of the effect.

9. Finally, open the **Light** menu and select, for example, the **Right** option.

10. Press the **OK** button to apply the effect and have a look at the result.

IMPORTANT

You can also obtain a crack effect if you use the **Craquelure** filter of the Texture category.

The images that are loaded to create new textures always have to be in **Photoshop's own format.**

Creating a water reflection

THERE ARE DIFFERENT TECHNIQUES that help you to reflect an object or a part of a photograph in the water. In this exercise, we will show you a simple method, which consists of copying the object or the part you want to reflect and vertically flipping it, which you will then to place on the right spot of the image.

1. Open the image you want to work with in Photoshop. In this case, you need a picture that does not display any reflections in a river or a sea (this effect with no reflections usually occurs on a cloudy day). If you do not have any images with these characteristics available, you can use sample file **080.jpg**.

2. Enable the **Rectangular Marquee Tool** 🔲 and draw a selection that covers the part or the object of the photograph you want to reflect in the water. (If you work with the sample file, select the ship.) 🔲

3. Copy the selection and paste it into a new layer. Press the key combination **Ctrl + C** and create a new layer by clicking on the **Create a new layer** icon in the **Layers** panel. 🔲

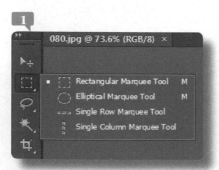

To begin the process, select the part of the image that you want to reflect in the water with an appropriate tool.

In Photoshop CS6, as you make a selection, a **tag** appears with the dimensions of it.

You can also create layers by using the **New Layer** option in the Layers panel or in the Layer menu or by clicking on **Shift + Ctrl + N**.

4. With the new layer selected, press the key combination **Ctrl + V** to paste the selected object in it.

5. Orient the pasted object properly in order to realize the reflection. Keep **Layer 1** selected, open the **Edit** menu, click on the **Transform** command and select the **Flip Vertical** option.

6. The object is now upside down and the original image has been hidden. You only need to orient it correctly and reduce the opacity of the layer to achieve the desired effect. Select the **Move Tool** in the **Tools** panel and drag the object on Layer 1 until it is placed correctly under the object of the **Background** layer.

7. If you have also selected a part of the background as you select the object, it can interfere with the composition and create an undesired effect. You can use the **Clone Stamp** and **Healing Brush Tool** to fix this problem. (Take an accurate sample of the Background layer and apply it to Layer 1.)

8. Reduce the opacity of Layer 1 to approximately **50%** (or the amount necessary to achieve your desired effect) and see how easily and quickly you have achieved an excellent reflection in the sea.

9. Open the **Options** menu of the **Layers** panel and click on the **Flatten image** command to merge the two layers into one.

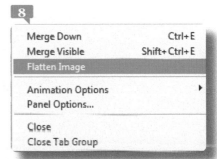

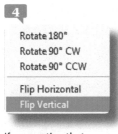

If you notice that the background of a selection can interfere negatively with the result of the reflection, try to select the object with more accuracy and without the background by means of the **Magic Wand** or **Quick Selection Tools**.

Creating panoramic images

SOME DIGITAL CAMERAS INCLUDE an option that is especially designed to take panoramic photographs. If this option is not available, you can create panoramas using the tools and utilities of Photoshop. It is important to keep certain aspects in mind while taking the photograph: the usage of a tripod and the overlap of the different shots needs to be at least 15%. Keeping a baseline is very important if you want to obtain optimal results.

1. If you would like, you can use our sample files **081-001.jpg** and **081-002.jpg**. Open the first image, which will serve as a panorama and which occupies the left part, in Photoshop (if you are using our sample files, open image **081-001.jpg**).

2. You need to increase the width of the image of the canvas, so that your two images will fit. As you only use two files in this exercise, you need to double the size of the canvas. Open the **Image** menu and click on the **Canvas Size** command. 🔲

3. In the **Canvas Size** dialog box, enter in the **Width** field the value that doubles the current width 🔲 (you can recall this size in the **Current Size** section of the dialog box).

4. If you now click on the **OK** button, the new dimensions will

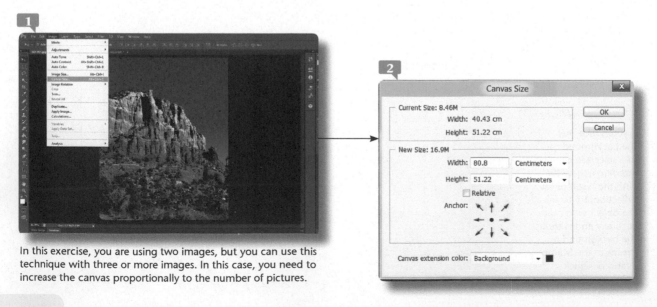

In this exercise, you are using two images, but you can use this technique with three or more images. In this case, you need to increase the canvas proportionally to the number of pictures.

081

be distributed on both sides of the canvas, adjusting the image in the center. Since you want to maintain the first picture on the left side of the canvas, select the **Relative** check box, and in the **Anchor** field, click on the left center cursor.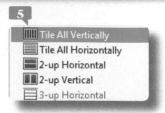

5. Now, press the **OK** button and have a look at the change in the dimensions of the canvas.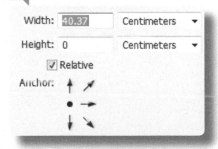

6. Open the second image, which becomes a part of the panorama.

7. Open the **Window** menu, click the **Arrange** command and select the **Tile All Vertically** option.

8. Select the **Move Tool** in the **Tools** panel.

9. It is important that the overlapping areas occupy the borders of the images of a panorama. Drag the second image until it is placed in the white part of the canvas of the first image.

10. In order to obtain the perfect overlap, it would be best if the Opacity of the second layer is temporarily decreased, so that you can see both images simultaneously and easily overlap the coinciding parts. Once you have carried out the adjustment, close the second image to have a look at the result.

The black spot of the **Anchor** tool indicates the position that the image occupies as you modify the dimensions of the canvas.

Width:	40.37	Centimeters ▼
Height:	0	Centimeters ▼
	☑ Relative	
Anchor:		

Apart from reducing the opacity of the layer, you can use the mouse and the arrow keys on your keyboard to adjust the two images perfectly.

Tile All Vertically
Tile All Horizontally
2-up Horizontal
2-up Vertical
3-up Horizontal

If you can see the canvas background as you create a panorama, use the **Crop Tool** to crop the image.

Creating panoramas automatically

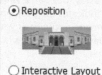
THE AUTOMATIZE COMMAND IN THE FILE MENU contains the Photomerge option, which allows you to combine several photographs into one panoramic image. After you have selected the images you want to use for the panorama, the program automatically tries to create a composition, using the colors and the values of the document as a reference. The composition can consist of different types of images and once created, it can be saved in the Photoshop format.

1. For this exercise, you need two images that contain two parts of a continuous landscape. (You can use the sample image of the previous exercise if you'd like.) You can combine the images in two ways: you can either open the images you want to merge or you can access the Photomerge dialog box and select the files there. To begin, open the **File** menu, click on the **Automatize** command and select the **Photomerge** option.

2. If you have previously opened the original images in the Photoshop workspace (you always need to open the files in the order you want to add them to the composition), the name of the files will now appear in the Photomerge box. Click on the **Browse** button. ▣

3. In the **Open** dialog box, locate and select the first image of

The **Photomerge** option allows you to combine horizontally or vertically segmented photographs to obtain panoramic images.

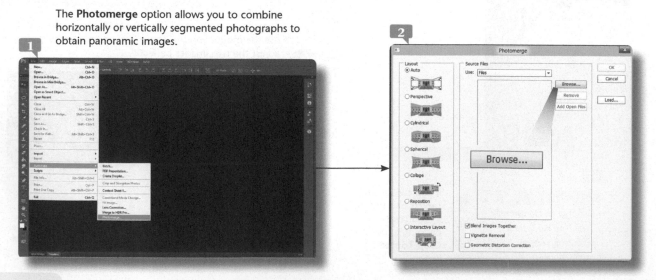

your composition and press the **OK** button.

4. Go back to the **Photomerge** dialog box, press the **Browse** button and repeat the steps above to open the second image as well.

5. Note that the Photomerge Tool offers different modes of composition. If you hold down the **Blend Images Together** option, the program will search for the optimal binding edges between images, and their colors will match perfectly. Keep the **Automatic** composition mode selected and click on **OK** to continue.

6. The program analyzes the content of the two images you want to connect and automatically and almost perfectly merges them in one continuous image. The two images that form the panorama occupy two different layers to which Photoshop has automatically added the necessary layer masks for the perfect fusion. Thus, if you need to retouch them, you can do it separately. Now you need to save the composition in Photoshop's own format. Open the **File** menu and click on the **Save** option.

7. Select the Photoshop format in the **Format** field, enter a name for the file, and click on the **Save** button.

082

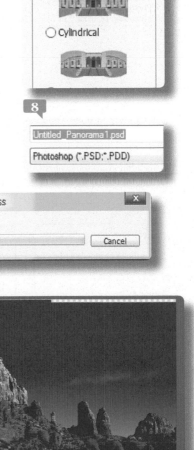

If you can see the canvas background as you create a panorama, use the Crop Tool to crop the image.

Photomerge adds **layer masks** to each of the layers of the composition of the panorama.

Creating object movies

IMPORTANT

Once you have created the animation, try to change the order and the duration of the shots, and, save it in the **GIF** format as you obtain the desired result.

Photoshop (*.PSD;*.PDD)
Large Document Format (*.PSB)
BMP (*.BMP;*.RLE;*.DIB)
CompuServe GIF (*.GIF)
Dicom (*.DCM;*.DC3;*.DIC)
Photoshop EPS (*.EPS)
Photoshop DCS 1.0 (*.EPS)

AN OBJECT MOVIE CONSISTS OF a sequence of images and is suitable, for example, for the presentation of a product on a Web page. Photoshop allows you to create non-interactive movies, which do not allow the viewer to control the display or movement of the movie. Once you have taken the images you want to use for the virtual movie, you need to access the Animation panel and add the pictures as shots.

1. Create a folder named **Movie**, which contains the files you want to use to create the movie (you can also use sample files **081-001.jpg** to **081-004.jpg**). Once you have that folder, you need to create a layer with each of the images in a new document by opening the **File** menu, clicking on the **Scripts** option and selecting **Load Files into Stack**.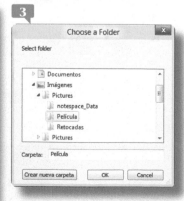

2. In the **Load Layers** box of the **Use** field, select the **Folder** option.

3. Click on the **Browse** button, locate and select your **Movie** folder in the **Choose Folder** box.

4. Now, all files of the folder are displayed. Enable the **Attempt to Automatically Align Source Images** option and press **OK**.

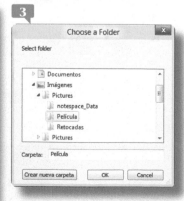

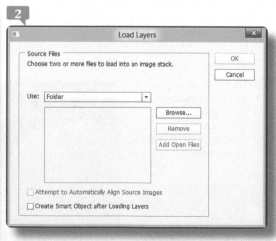

You can choose to upload individual files or upload an entire folder.

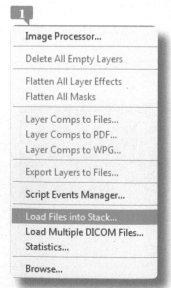

Your job as a **movie** creator will be much easier if you have a folder with all the files in it.

5. In Photoshop CS6, the **Animation** panel opens by default at the bottom of the interface in the **Frames** mode. In order to display it as a timeline, click on the icon that appears in the lower right corner.

6. Click on the **Options** button and select **Document Settings**.

7. In the **Document Timeline Settings** box, you can define the length of the film and the image frequency. In this case, indicate that you want to display 5 shots per second by inserting the value **5** in the second **Frame Rate** field and press **OK**.

8. Now, you need to create a frame from each layer to obtain the animation. Open the **Options** menu of the **Animation** panel again and select the **Make Frames From Layers** option.

9. In order to check that you have created a frame for each layer, activate the **Frames** mode of the **Animation** panel by clicking on the icon on its bottom right.

10. To preview the animation, click on the **Plays Animation** button, which displays a cursor in the **Status** bar of the **Animation** panel.

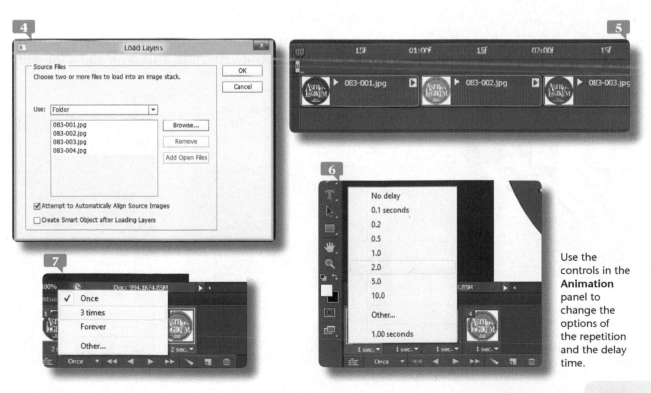

Use the controls in the **Animation** panel to change the options of the repetition and the delay time.

Converting a 2D image into a 3D image

IMPORTANT

With the help of the enhanced 3D objects editing tools, you can create sophisticated **3D animations** from the Animation panel, where you can control the movement of an object, the camera position, lighting effects, the application of textures, etc.

PHOTOSHOP CS6 ALLOWS YOU TO convert 2D objects into 3D ones. You can apply 2D image wrappings to common 3D geometric shapes such as pyramids, loops, spheres, spherical panoramas, etc., with very simple pre-adjustments. You can even convert gradient maps into 3D objects.

1. Start this exercise with a blank document of 400 by 400 pixels. On this document, you need to create a gradient map that will later become a 3D object. Click on the cursor of the **Paint Bucket Tool** and select the **Gradient Tool.** 🗨1

2. Click on the cursor button of the gradient sample in the **Options Bar** and select one of the available gradient samples by double-clicking on it. 🗨2

3. In order to apply the gradient to the bottom of the document, click on a point and drag it to another point. 🗨3

4. Once you have created a gradient map in the 3D panel, select the **Mesh from Preset** option, display the next field and select, for example, the **Soda** shape. 🗨4

5. Click on the **Create** button and check in the **Layers** panel if the bottom layer got converted into a 3D layer and if the edit-

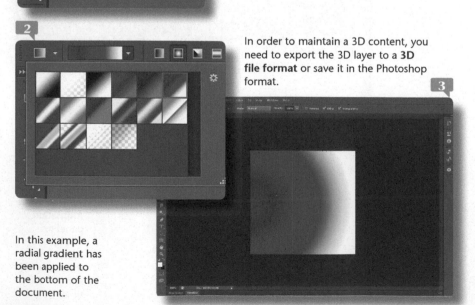

In this example, a radial gradient has been applied to the bottom of the document.

In order to maintain a 3D content, you need to export the 3D layer to a **3D file format** or save it in the Photoshop format.

084

ing options of the 3D object are already displayed in the 3D panel. [5]

6. Enable the **Move Tool** to load the 3D transformation tools in the **Options Bar**. Then select the **Rotate 3D Object Tool** [6] and drag the pointer on the image to check if the gradient map has been distributed as a label of the selected shape. [7]

7. Leave the new 3D interface by clicking on the Selection Tool and save the image.

8. Now open a JPG image of a landscape, which you have saved on your computer, in Photoshop (you can recover sample image **007.jpg**), open the **3D** menu, and then click on the **New Mesh from the layer** command, select the **Mesh preset** option and choose, for example, the **Sphere** shape. [8]

9. Use the **3D Rotation** and displacement tools to have a look at the effect. [9]

10. Finally, export the 3D layer you are working with to one of the available formats. Open the **3D** menu and click on the **Export 3D Layer** option.

11. Press the cursor button of the **Format** field, choose your own **Google Earth** and click on the **Save** button.

12. Keep the 3D export options that are displayed in the dialog box and click on **OK**.

The 3D objects can move in the 3D space and change the settings of render, lighting, materials, etc.

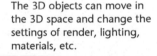

Rotate the 3D Object

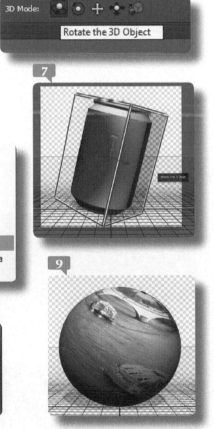

Cylinder
Donut
Hat
Pyramid
Ring
Soda
Sphere
Spherical Panorama
Wine Bottle

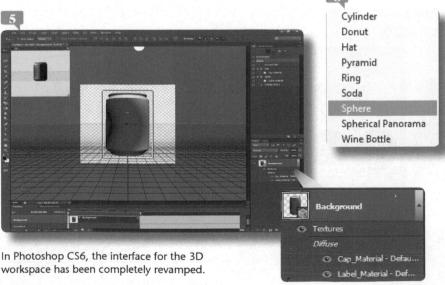

In Photoshop CS6, the interface for the 3D workspace has been completely revamped.

Applying 3D materials

IN THE PREVIOUS EXERCISE you saw the change in the Photoshop CS6 interface as you started working in 3D. In this exercise, you will have a look at the functioning of the two new tools that help you to apply 3D materials: the 3D Material Drop and the 3D Material Eyedropper.

1. For this exercise, you need to use the two 3D documents (which you have created in the previous exercise), and which should be open. If they are not available, you can use sample images **084-001.psd** and **084-002.psd**, which can be found in the download area on our website. Let's get to know the functioning of the new **3D Material Drop Tool**. Go to the first image (the one with the can in it), display the **Gradient Tool** and select the **3D Material Drop Tool**. 🗨1

2. In the **Options Bar** you can check if you are not currently working with any 3D material. 🗨2 Open the box of the samples, have a look at the available materials, and double-click on one of them. 🗨3

3. The selected material is loaded into the program and is ready to be applied. Check if its name is now displayed in the

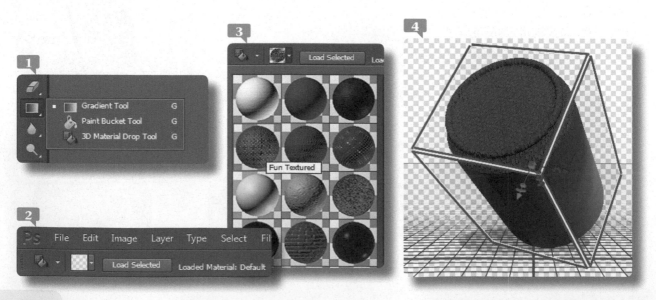

182

085

Options Bar. In order to apply the new material to the top of your soda can, click on this part of the image and have a look at the result. 4

4. Indeed, the selected material is applied to the designated part, omitting the part of the label. Now you need to select the material of the label and apply it to the sphere of the second document. In the 3D panel, select the material **Label_Material** and click on the **Load Selected** button in the **Options Bar.** 5

5. Have a look at the change in the field of samples of this bar as well as in the text that designates the currently loaded material. Place the second image into the foreground (the one with the sphere), check if the label material remains loaded, and click on the object.

6. The sphere now displays the gradient material. 6 The second tool, the **3D Material Eyedropper**, which we also want to explain in this exercise, works similar to the **3D Material Drop** tool. Open the **Eyedropper Tool**, which is the sixth icon in the **Tools** panel, and select the aforementioned new tool. 7

7. This tool works like the conventional droppers, such as the Fill tool or the paint bucket. Go back to the first document, take a sample of the material by clicking on the top of the can, return to the document of the sphere and, after selecting the new **3D Material Drop Tool**, fill the sphere with the sampled material. 8

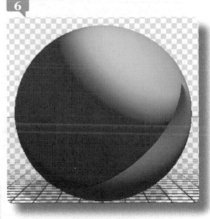

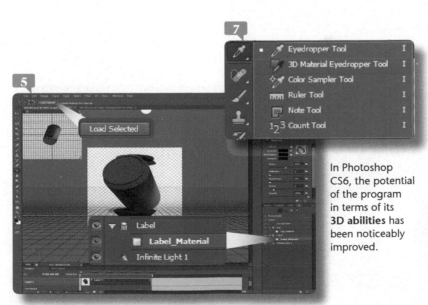

In Photoshop CS6, the potential of the program in terms of its **3D abilities** has been noticeably improved.

Adding text in 3D

AS YOU SAW IN THE PREVIOUS EXERCISES, Photoshop CS6 provides a new spectacular 3D function with a renewed interface to work with. The enhanced function also includes the extrusion of the text, and the point of view.

1. To begin, select the Horizontal Text Tool in the **Tools** panel and type a word on your image.

2. A new text layer will appear in the **Layers** panel. In the **Options Bar** or the **Character** panel, modify the text properties to achieve your desired result.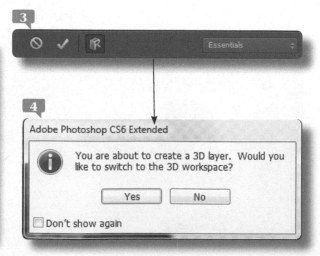

3. After confirming the insertion of the text, you will see an icon with a 3D **R** in the **Options Bar**. This icon and the 3D function are new in Photoshop CS6. Select the new text layer and click on this icon.  (If the icon does not appear in your interface, open the **Type** menu and click on the **Extrude to 3D** command.)

4. Then, a dialog box opens  that informs you that a 3D layer will be generated and that your permission is needed to switch to the new 3D workspace. Click on the **Yes** button and wait a few seconds until the 3D space has been loaded.

184

5. Apart from creating the new 3D layer, the image appears in a 3D space that allows you to manipulate it. Now, you will learn how to work with 3D text. In order to do this, rotate the image with the 3D rotation tool. By default, this tool is enabled in the **Options Bar** of the **3D Mode** section.

6. Note that the power of your computer will determine the speed of the 3D manipulation. With the help of the enabled icon in the **Options Bar**, you can rotate or revolve around the text, you can move it and even change its size. Each option is symbolized by a proper shaft or handle on the text in the image.

7. At the top of the screen you can see an incomplete white circle. Click on it and watch what happens.

8. In the center of the image appears a sphere that helps you to indicate the point from where the 3D text should be lit up. Move the smaller sphere located at the opposite end of the line, since it connects both spheres to direct the light the way you want it. When finished, click on the white circle again to deactivate the lighting option. (Note that this icon will have changed the position in the image.)

9. To exit the 3D space, select a different layer or a new tool.

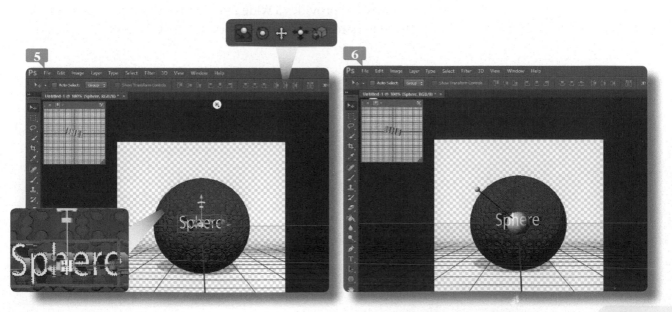

Adding watermarks to your photos

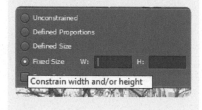

THE DISTRIBUTION AND EXHIBITION of digital images is usually the goal of professionals who dedicate themselves to the world of photography. Professionals promote their work by posting images online. The distribution of digital images involves a number of measures, which need to be taken into account to prevent the copying or misappropriation by others. Watermarks can be a good solution to prevent the misuse of distributed images.

1. Although distribution is not the main purpose of the images in the domestic field, it is the last step of professional photographic work. This is why, we have included two chapters on creating watermarks and copyright assignment. Creating a watermark is a design process. It is characterized by the usage of a symbol, text, or picture that is inserted into the image as a sign of ownership. To begin, open the file you want to retouch in Photoshop (you may use sample image **087.jpg**).

2. The symbol that you will insert into the image in this exercise is the copyright symbol. But if you prefer, you can use any other symbol to customize the exercise. In the **Tools** panel, enable the **Custom Shape Tool**, which is grouped with the other shape creation tools.

3. Photoshop provides a wide range of shapes that can be added to images to create a watermark. In the **Options Bar**, click on

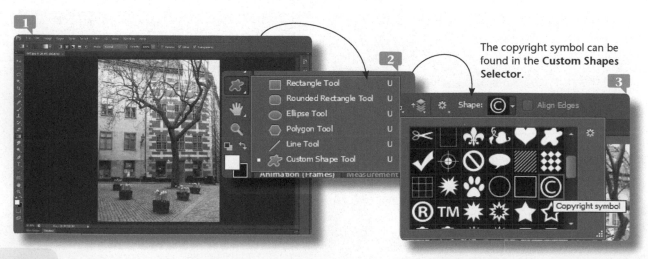

The copyright symbol can be found in the **Custom Shapes Selector**.

the cursor of the **Shape** field, then find the copyright symbol in the Custom Shape Selector and double-click on it.

4. Click on the **Create a new layer** icon in the **Layers** panel, make sure that the foreground color is black and that the **Pixels** option is enabled in the **Options Bar**. Click anywhere on the image and drag the symbol until you obtain the dimensions you want.

5. You need to apply an embossed effect to the symbol. Open the **Filter** menu, click on the **Stylize** command and select the **Emboss** filter.

6. In the **Emboss** window, change the Angle, Height, and Amount until you achieve the desired effect and click on **OK** to apply it.

7. Finally, in the **Layers** panel, reduce the Opacity of the layer to increase the transparency of the symbol in the image.

8. Now, your image features its corresponding watermark. To finish this exercise, connect the image by using the appropriate option in the emergent menu of the **Layers** panel.

087

You can also add a **Gaussian Blur,** which would give it a smoother shape.

Adding copyright to images

THIS EXERCISE SHOWS YOU how to add author-related information to a photograph, such us information about the copyright. Including this information ensures that the related data of the file ownership appears on the Web in the case that someone uses the photograph without the permission of the owner. The copyright information is not displayed on the image (as in the case of the watermarks), but this data is attached to the image file information.

1. You can use any photo for this exercise. It is important to know that the copyright information is supported by the most common file formats (such as TIFF, JPEG, EPS, PDF, and the PSD Photoshop format) in Windows, whereas Macintosh supports them all. To begin, open the image in the workspace, go to the **File** menu and click on the **File Info** command.

2. In the dialog box that automatically opens, you should enter all picture-related information with reference to its authorship. There is no need to complete all available fields, just the ones that seems to be appropriate. Go to the **Description** tab, open the **Copyright Status** field, which will display the term **Unknown**, and select the option **Copyrighted**.

3. Then click the **Copyright Notice** field and type in any text you want to warn those who want to use your image, for example on a website.

4. The **Copyright Info URL** field allows you to add the image owner's website address. Thus, all people who will open the file information box, can access the website of the author by clicking on the **Go To URL** button. If you have a personal website that displays your work, feel free to make yourself known by filling in this field.

5. At the top of the dialog box you can find the fields in which the author-related information of the picture will appear. If you want to, you can add the data you find interesting to the file information. You can also add a description of the photo, sort it by star ratings, enter keywords that will help you to locate it, etc. At the bottom of the box, you can find the creation date and the format of the image. If you do not want to add any further information, press the **OK** button.

6. The sign, which indicates that the photograph contains copyright information, is now visible in the file tab, right before the title of the image as well as in its **Status Bar,** together with the document size. You can finish this exercise by saving the changes.

The metadata, which is added to the table of the file information, is stored in the standard **Extensible Metadata Platform (XMP)**.

Creating a copyright brush

IN ORDER TO APPLY THE COPYRIGHT information quickly and easily to your photograph, you can convert this information into a custom brush that you can use anytime as you would any other brush.

1. Open one of your pictures in Photoshop and create a new blank canvas.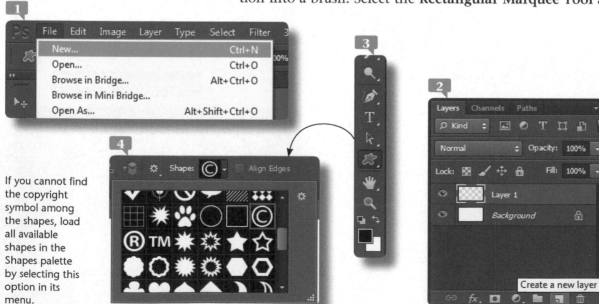

2. Add a blank layer by clicking on the **Create a new layer** icon in the **Layers** panel.

3. Select the **Custom Shape Tool** in the **Tools** panel, check if the **Pixels** option is enabled in the **Options Bar**, go to the Shapes palette and select with a double-click the copyright symbol.

4. Draw by dragging the symbol into the blank document, enable the **Horizontal Type Tool** and write next to the symbol the copyright information you want to display in your photograph.

5. See how the text layer places itself above the one that contains the copyright symbol. Now you need to convert this information into a brush. Select the **Rectangular Marquee Tool** and

If you cannot find the copyright symbol among the shapes, load all available shapes in the Shapes palette by selecting this option in its menu.

190

draw a selection that covers all the information.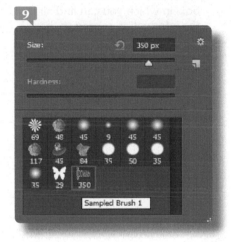

6. Open the **Edit** menu and click on the **Define Brush Preset** option.

7. Name your copyright brush in the **Brush Name** box and click on the **OK** button.

8. After you have created the brush, close the new document without saving the changes in order to go back to your picture.

9. Click on the **Create a new layer** icon in the **Layers** panel to add a blank layer to the document.

10. Enable the **Brush Tool** in the **Tools** panel and, in the **Brush** selector of the **Options Bar**, locate and select with a double-click the custom brush that you have just created.

11. The brush is loaded and ready to be applied to the image. Click anywhere you want to display the copyright information.

12. Now you just need to decrease the Opacity of the layer and apply a filter (such as **Emboss** or **Gaussian Blur**) to enhance the effect. Reduce the Opacity of this layer and have a look at the effect.

Note that, depending on the image you want to apply the copyright brush to, you should use one color for the copyright and another one for the text, so it is visible.

Using the Digimarc filter for copyright protection

IMPORTANT

In order to recall the data of the digital copyright you should use the **Read Watermark** option of the Digimarc filter. In this way, you can access the Watermark Information box, in which you can find all the information related to the image.

Embed Watermark...
Read Watermark...

PHOTOSHOP PROVIDES A WAY to embed copyright information into the created files. It is called Digimarc, a digital copyright watermark that requires the user to pay an annual subscription to the company providing this service. The Digimarc file information, as described above, is not visible on the image, but the information still travels with the image. To use a Digimarc, you need to implement it before the file is stored, and the layers in the file need to be flattened.

1. This exercise shows you what you have to do if you want to apply a digital copyright to your images. To do this, you can use any image. Open the photograph in the Photoshop workspace.

2. The digital copyright Digimarc is included as a filter in Photoshop. So open the **Filter** menu, click on the **Digimarc** command and select **Embed Watermark**.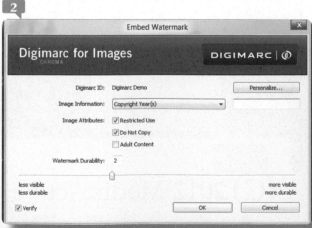

3. As already indicated, the use of Digimarc requires an annual subscription to this service that can be completed in the **Embed Watermark** box.  The service provides a Digimarc ID and PIN to the user. This data needs to be entered within the subscription process. Press the **Personalize** button.

4. In the **Personalize Digimarc ID** table, you should enter the data mentioned in the previous step. If you have not

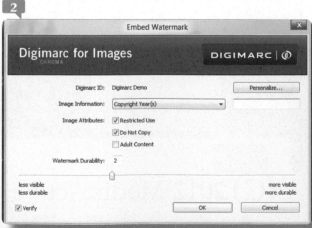

090

subscribed to the service, you need to access the website www.digimarc.com/register and follow the steps. Once registered, you will obtain the necessary ID and PIN to use Digimarc. Insert them into the appropriate fields and click on **OK**. ⬛

5. Back in the **Embed Watermark** box, enter the photo's copyright year in the Image Information section (you can also select other data if you display the list). ⬛

6. In the **Image Attributes** section, check the boxes corresponding to the information that you want to display in the picture (you can choose between **Restricted Use**, **Do Not Copy**, and **Adult Content**—you can select all or none of them). ⬛

7. Adjust the Watermark Strength by using the slider at the bottom of the dialog box, select the **Verify** option and press the **OK** button.

8. With the **Verify** option enabled, the service checks the intensity of the watermark on the image and if the process has been completed successfully. ⬛ Click on the **OK** button to finish the process.

9. See if the copyright symbol appears in the tab of the image, ⬛ while the remaining information is embedded into the file. Now you can save the image with the new feature.

If your image is in JPEG format, you should store it with a **compression quality higher than 4**, otherwise, the watermark cannot be kept in the file.

Adding information to images

THE METADATA OF A FILE consist of different types of information that facilitate the work flow as well as the organization of the files. The most common metadata are the author's name of the file, the resolution, the color space, the copyright of the image (which you have seen before), the camera data, the customized metadata, etc. There are, however, many other types of data that can be inserted into the File Info box.

1. Open any photo in the Photoshop workspace, go to the **File** menu and select the **File Info** option.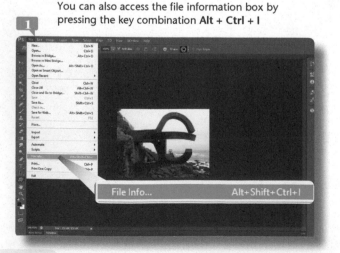

2. The **File Info** box is where the categories of the file information are displayed. As you can see, they are subdivided into different groups. In the **Description** category, enter the basic data of the file (name, author, description, keywords that will help you to locate it). Remember that in this category you can find the option that allows you to add the copyright information. Name your photograph in the **Document Title** field, and add a brief description of the document in the **Description** field.

3. Enter keywords that should be separated by commas, which will help you find the file more easily in the **Keywords** field.

You can also access the file information box by pressing the key combination **Alt + Ctrl + I**

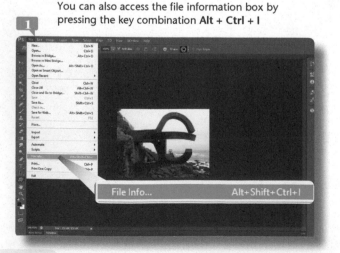

091

4. In the remaining categories, you can add write-protected information about the camera, the settings you used when you took the photo, as well as the photo itself. Further, you can add information based on the categories of the Associated Press, registration information about the Photoshop history of the saved images, digital image metadata (such as contact information of the photographer), visual content of the images, and information of the work flow and copyright, etc. Click on the cursor button that appears on the right of the tab, and then click on the category **DICOM**.

5. The standard **DICOM** (*Digital Imaging and Communication in Medicine*) is used worldwide for the exchange of medical images. In this section, you can enter all types of medical data about the image. Depending on the file you are working with, there may be additional information categories such as audio and video. Click on the **Origin** tab.

6. In this section, you can add useful information for the publication of news, such as date and place of the creation of the file, information owners, degree of urgency, etc. Click on the icon next to the **Date Created** field and select the current date in the calendar.

7. Display the options of the **Import** button, select the **Export** option, enter a name in the **Export** box and click on **Save**.

8. Press the **OK** button to add the information to the file and thereby finish this exercise.

DICOM is the most commonly used standard to exchange medical information.

- ✔ Description
- ✔ IPTC
- ✔ IPTC Extension
- ✔ Camera Data
- ✔ GPS Data
- ✔ Video Data
- ✔ Audio Data
- ✔ Mobile SWF
- ✔ Categories
- ✔ Origin
- ✔ DICOM
- ✔ History
- ✔ Advanced
- ✔ Raw Data

By default, the file information is saved in a Photoshop folder called **Metadata Templates** and in the format **.xmp**. If you want to, you can select any other location on your computer.

Viewing a slideshow

IMPORTANT

In order to view all files in the **Open** dialog box (regardless of their format) keep the **All formats** option in the **Type** field selected. If you want to display a particular format, select it in this field.

THERE ARE MANY APPLICATIONS ON THE MARKET that are designed to display collections of images on your computer. However, as this book displays the features of Photoshop CS6 in order to retouch photos, this exercise will describe different techniques with which you can use this program as an excellent image viewer. Once you have downloaded and retouched the photographs, you may want to show them to your friends, family, or colleagues.

1. In this simple exercise, you will see how to create a presentation of your photograph collections by using Photoshop. The first thing you need to do is open all images you want to display. To do this, open the **File** menu and click on the **Open** command. 🔳

2. In the **Open** dialog box, find the folder or location of your material and double-click on it to display its contents. 🔳

3. You probably already know that if you want to select a sequence of consecutive images at once, you just need to click on the first and last picture while holding the **Shift** key down. If, on the other hand, you want to select pictures in a random order, you need to select them by clicking on them

Remember you can also access the **Open** dialog box by pressing the key combination **Ctrl + O** on your keyboard.

You can change the display mode of the files in the **Open** window using the last icon in its toolbar.

092

and holding the **Ctrl** key down. Select the images you wish to open and click the **Open** button.

4. The images open and each picture occupies a corresponding document window. Click for a few seconds on the last icon of the **Tools** panel and select the **Full Screen Mode** option.

5. Read the information that appears and go to the full screen view by pressing the **Full Screen** button.

6. A multitude of changes are immediately carried out in the work area: the current image is shown on a black background and all toolbars and palettes have been hidden (the latter can be displayed if you move the cursor to the left and right margin). Now you just need to move the photographs. Press the key combination **Ctrl + Tab** to jump to the next image.

7. The next image is also shown on a black background, outside of the document window. In order to move to the next image, press the key combination **Ctrl + Tab**. Repeat this as many times as necessary.

8. When you have finished the slideshow, press the **Escape** key or the **F** key to return to the normal screen mode and, finally, select the menu path **File/Close All** to close all images.

You can find these display options in the **Screen Mode** submenu of the View menu.

197

Creating layer compositions

LAYER COMPOSITIONS ALLOW YOU to display different states of the photographs you are retouching in a single Photoshop file. They are snapshots of the state of the Layers panel and especially used to display compositions to customers.

1. Open any photograph in Photoshop and realize any change on it, for example, apply the Hue/Saturation adjustment layer to display it in sepia tone. Open the **Window** menu and click on **Layer Comps** to display this panel.

2. In the **Layer Comps** panel click on the fourth icon called **Create new layer comp.**

3. In the **New Layer Comp** box, give the composition a name, set the attributes you want Photoshop to remember and add a brief description. Type in a name for your first composition, enable the **Visibility**, **Position,** and **Appearance** options, add a comment and click on the **OK** button.

4. You already obtained the first composition in the panel. Now you can restore the actual appearance of your pictures even after making the modifications. Add another effect to the image

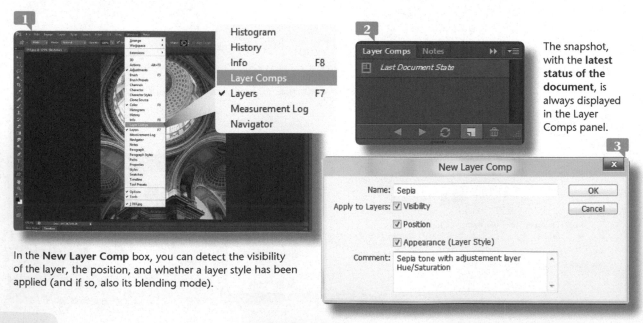

The snapshot, with the **latest status of the document**, is always displayed in the Layer Comps panel.

In the **New Layer Comp** box, you can detect the visibility of the layer, the position, and whether a layer style has been applied (and if so, also its blending mode).

(for example, you can create a plasticized effect if you follow the steps of the corresponding exercise in this book).

5. Create a new layer composition and adjust its properties in the **New Layer Comp** box.

6. Repeat the procedure for each retouching step in order to obtain different states of the image and see how they are added (with the corresponding comment) to the **Layer Comps** panel.

7. To move one composition to another, use the cursor buttons at the bottom of the panel.

8. Go to the first layer composition by clicking on the gray box that appears on your left and make another change, such as an adjustment of the hue, saturation, or brightness. In order to display the change in your composition, click on the **Update Layer Comp** icon, which is the third one at the bottom of the panel.

9. In order to remove a layer composition, you simply need to select it and click on the last icon in the panel. If you want to modify the options of a layer composition, just double-click on it and select the **Layer Comp Options** command in the Options menu of the panel to access the Properties box.

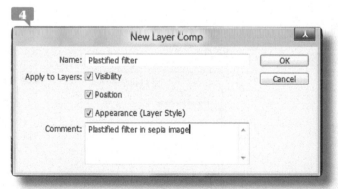

As in the other panels, all actions that are carried out by the panel icons, can be complited in their Options menu.

Creating a contact sheet

THE CONTACT SHEET creates a number of thumbnail previews on a page that can be printed. The thumbnails can be a specified size or the size of the contact sheet. In addition, by using the Contact Sheet II box, you can distribute the thumbnails in the necessary number of columns and rows. Each thumbnail displays the corresponding file name at the bottom. In case the number of images exceeds the number of thumbnails established by the columns and rows, a new contact sheet with the remaining images will be created automatically.

1. Use a folder that contains several of the images you worked on in these exercises. To begin, open the **File** menu, click on the **Automate** command and select the **Contact Sheet II** option. 1

2. In the **Contact Sheet II** box, you need to define the images that you want for your contact sheet. Press the **Choose** button in the **Source Images** section, 2 locate and select your folder in the **Choose a Folder** box and click on **OK**. 3

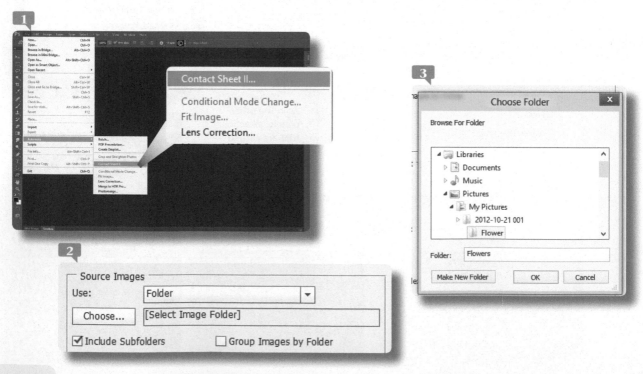

3. Define the number of columns and rows in the Thumbnails section. Enter the value of **3** in both fields. [4]

4. Click on the check box of the **Include Subfolders** option of the **Source Images** section in order to disable it. [5]

5. Make sure that the **Use Filename as Caption** section to label the thumbnails using their source image file names is checked. If you wish, you can define a different font and size other than the default ones [6] or even disable this option. Click on **OK**.

6. After the import, which can take a while depending on the content of your folder, Photoshop automatically generates the documents with the thumbnails in them. Each thumbnail appears with the corresponding file name. [7]

7. You need to see the contact sheet in its actual size. Open the **View** menu and select the **Actual Pixels** option. [8]

8. Click on the close button of the tab of the contact sheet and press the **Yes** button that appears in the box.

9. Give a name to the sheet, select the storage location and click on the **Save** button. Repeat it with the other sheets.

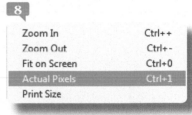

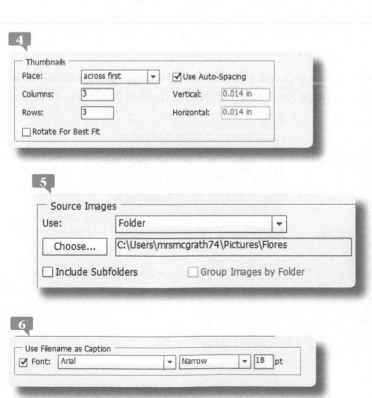

Photoshop treats each contact sheet as a separate document that can be saved as you would any other document.

Recording and playing an action

AN ACTION IS A SET OF COMMANDS that is carried out on a file or a batch of files. The actions are saved in the Actions panel. Photoshop offers a number of preset actions. The actions can consist of one or several steps. Any command can be an action and, if you want to, can be assigned to a function key (F1, F2, F3. . .) After creating the actions, you can add or remove steps with the Create New Action or Delete commands.

1. In this exercise, you will create an action to expand the size of an image. Open any photo in Photoshop, go to the **Window** menu and select the **Actions** option.

2. In the **Actions** panel, select the **Default Actions** group and click on the **Create new action** icon (the next to last panel).

3. Type, for example, the word **Increase** in the **Name** field of the **New Action** box.

4. Apply a function key to carry out the new action by simply pressing that key. Open the menu of the **Function Key** field and select **F2**. Then, click on the **Record** button to begin storing of the steps.

5. In the **Actions** panel you can see that the name of the new action is displayed next to the assigned function key. An

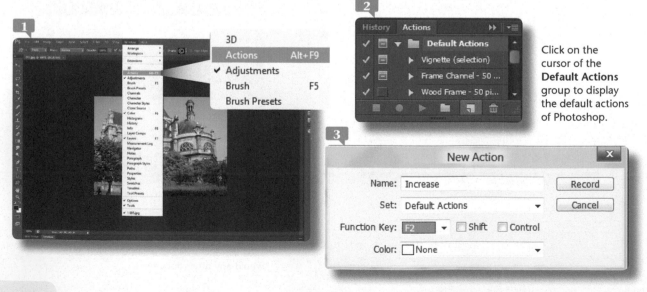

Click on the cursor of the **Default Actions** group to display the default actions of Photoshop.

icon with a red circle appears, which indicates that each action that you will carry out from now on will be recorded. To begin with the the steps required for this action, open the **Image** menu and select the **Image Size** option.

6. Enable the **Resample Image** option if it is disabled, open the field that appears below this option and select **Bicubic Smoother**.

7. Then in the **Width** field of the **Document Size** section, change **Centimeters** (or the one you are using right now) to **Percent**

8. Remember that if the increase of the image dimensions is carried out by using a 10% increase, no quality will be lost, whereas higher values for width and height will cause a blur and fade effect. Enter a valuc of **110** in the **Width** field and accept the changes.

9. Press the button **Stop Playing/Recording**, which is the first one in the **Actions** panel.

10. After creating the action, use it out on a new image by pressing the assigned function key. Open another image and press the **F2** key.

See how the image size increases by 10%. You can keep on increasing the size by pressing the **F2** key as many times as you want.

IMPORTANT

Avoid assigning an action to a **keyboard shortcut** that is already used as a command, because then the keyboard shortcut will be used for the action rather than for the aforesaid command.

In order to carry out an action that has been assigned to a function key, it is not necessary that it is selected in the Actions panel.

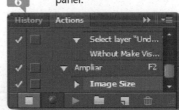

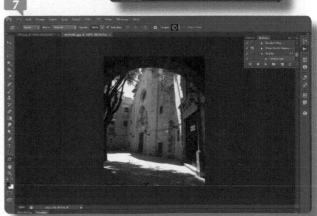

Playing actions on batches of images

ACTIONS CAN AUTOMATICALLY BE APPLIED to a group of images, a file folder, or a subfolder using the Batch option. In the Batch dialog box, you need to define the group that contains the image, action, and folder or unit in which you can find the images or files you want to modify. You can even access an external unit (such as a digital camera or scanner) and apply a certain action.

1. Before starting this exercise, create a folder with various images and name it **Batch**. Once you have done this, open the **File** menu, click on the **Automate** command and select the **Batch** option.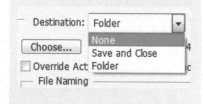

2. In the **Batch** box you need to select the group that contains the action you want to apply. Strictly speaking, you want to increase the size of the images by 10%. You have already created this action in the previous exercise within the **Default Actions** group. Select this action and select the **Increase** option in the **Action** field.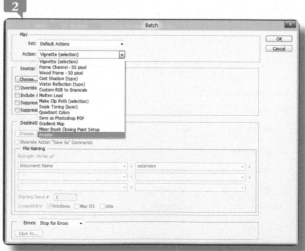

3. Select the origin of the images. If you want to use a multitude of images taken with a digital camera or captured in a scanner, you need to select the Import option in this field and follow

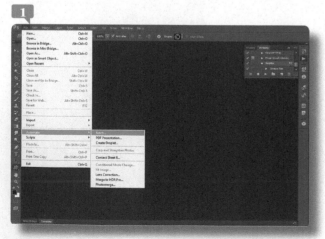

The **Batch** command allows you to carry out a selected action in the file folder, which is defined by its same name in the box.

The menus of the Batch box display the sets and actions included in the **Actions** panel.

the instructions of the program. In this case, keep the **Folder** option in the **Source** field and click on the **Choose** button.

4. In the **Search** folder, find and select your **Batch** folder and click on **OK**.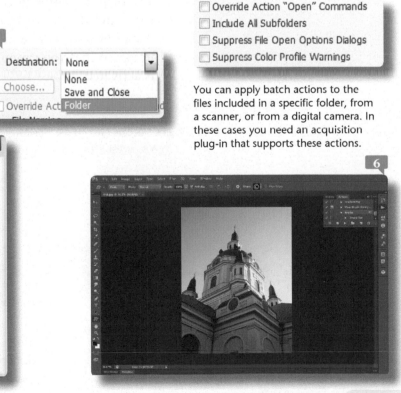

5. If one of the steps of the action is open, you can omit it by activating the **Override Action "Open" Commands** option in order to simplify the process. Once you have determined the action you want to apply and where the images you want to convert are located, you need to save the remaining images in a folder. Open the **Destination** field and select the **Folder** option.

6. Press the **Choose** button in the **Destination** section and locate and select the destination folder in the **Search** folder.

7. Define the properties of the batch and click on **OK** to confirm the process.

All images in the selected folder open automatically one by one, and the indicated action is applied to the pictures. Finish the exercise by opening the previously selected destination folder in order to check if the images have been saved correctly with their new dimensions.

4

☐ Override Action "Open" Commands
☐ Include All Subfolders
☐ Suppress File Open Options Dialogs
☐ Suppress Color Profile Warnings

You can apply batch actions to the files included in a specific folder, from a scanner, or from a digital camera. In these cases you need an acquisition plug-in that supports these actions.

5

Destination: None ▼
    None
Choose...   Save and Close
☐ Override Act Folder

3

Buscar carpeta ✕

Choose a batch folder...

◢ 📚 Bibliotecas
  ▷ 🎵 Música
  ▷ 🎬 Vídeos
  ▷ 📄 Documentos
  ◢ 🖼 Imágenes
    ◢ 📁 Pictures
        📁 Flores
        📁 Lote
        📁 notespace_Data
        📁 Película
        📁 Retocadas

Aceptar   Cancelar

Printing photos

IN ORDER TO PRINT DIGITAL PHOTOGRAPHS at home, you need to consider several things go beyond simply clicking on the Print command. One of the most important aspects is the use of a good ink printer. The downside is that it is a process that can be expensive due to the cost of ink and photographic printing paper.

1. Open an image with an aspect ratio of 3:2 (as in sample file **097.jpg**) in Photoshop, open the **File** menu and click on the **Print** command.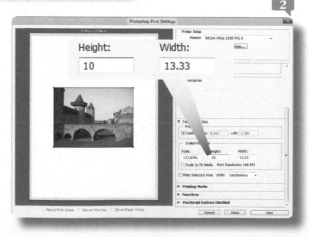

2. By default, the **Center** option is checked in the **Position and Size** section and thus, the image is located in the center of the page. The print size is displayed in the **Scaled Print Size** section. You can manually enter the size of the image you want to print. In order to do this, the option **Scale to Fit Media** needs to be disabled. As an example, enter in the **Height** field a value of **10.**

3. The height is automatically adjusted to the equivalent width, since the dimensions are proportional. The **Print Selected Area** option applies a margin with four drawing tools on the image so that you can modify its size. Check if this option is activated.

3

☑ Print Selected Area   Units: Centimeters ▼

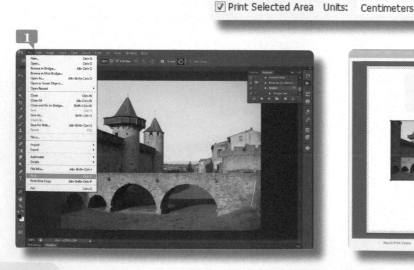

Height: 10   Width: 13.33

4. If you need to adjust the parameters for the edge, bottom, and indention, you should go to the **Functions** section, and you can find the options for the printing marks of the document in the **Printing Marks** section. 🔲

5. In the **Printer Setup** section click on the second icon to the right of the **Layout** field to display the image horizontally. 🔲

6. The paper size and type, and other aspects directly related to the printer, can also be configured in this table. Click on the **Print Settings** button. 🔲

7. Since you have already worked with this table many times, you already know that from here you can change the orientation of the paper and its size. Adjust these parameters according to the image you are using in this exercise, set the options of your printer and click on **OK**. 🔲

8. Select the printer you want to use in the **Printer** field of the **Photoshop Print Settings** box. The properties, which appear in the Page Adjustment box, will be adjusted for the printer. In this box, you can find, among others, the option to choose the paper type you want to use for your printing. After ensuring that your printer is properly connected to the computer and turned on, click on the **Print** button to obtain your printed copy.

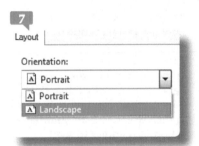

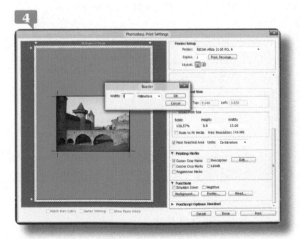

In the Properties box, you can adjust the aspects directly related to the printer, such as size, color, print quality, etc.

Autosave in Photoshop CS6

MANY PHOTOSHOP USERS missed the ability to configure an autosave function to protect them from accidentally losing their work (due to a system failure, a voltage drop, etc.). Photoshop CS6 now includes this feature in its preferences window, specifically in the File Management category. Furthermore, it allows you to add optional plugins such as PSDAutoSaver, by the Electric Iris company, with which you can configure other advanced autosave options.

1. Assume you have been working on a picture for some time now and that you have added several effects and that it is composed of several layers. In previous versions of Photoshop, if you forgot to save your file regularly, you ran the risk of losing all the information on the picture if the system was shut down unexpectedly. Now, you can configure the program to save you documents automatically. You will now learn how it's done. Open the **Edit** menu, click on the **Preferences** option and choose **File Handling**.

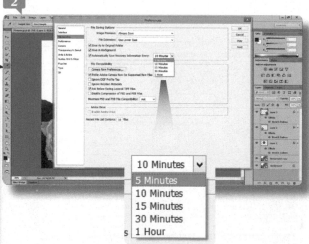

Adobe ha añadido una función de autoguardado en Photoshop CS6 para evitar pérdidas accidentales de sus proyectos.

Lógicamente, en función del tamaño del archivo con el que esté trabajando, la función de autoguardado puede hacer más lenta la actividad del programa.

2. Notice that, in the **File Sharing Options** section, a new option is available in this version of the program: **Automatically Save Recovery Information Every.** You can configure this feature by specifying the number of minutes that suits you best. Keep the option on, click on the arrow button in the field that displays the date and time and choose, for instance, **5 minutes.**

3. With this feature, Photoshop creates a temporary file you can recover, that contains the latest information on the picture you are editing. If you uncheck the autosave box, you will need to save you file manually every time. Click on the **OK** button to accept the new preferences.

4. Apart from using this autosave function, you can also add some of the many new plugins available for Photoshop CS6 to make your job easier. One of these plugins is **PSDAutosaver.** Once you have downloaded this plugin's trial version from the Electric Iris website, you will be able to find it in the menu path **File/Automate/PsdAutoSaver.**

5. This will open the program's settings window, where you can enable or disable the function, set the interval at which you want your work to be saved, to which file size you want to apply the autosave, in which folder you want to save your security copies, how many files you wish to maintain in your history, and how often they must be deleted. Configure this plugin according to your preferences.

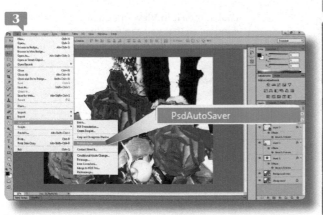

Los plugins que añada a Photoshop se mostrarán en la ruta de menú correspondiente según la función que llevan a cabo en el programa. En este caso, puesto que se trata de una acción automática, se añade al submenú Automate del menú File.

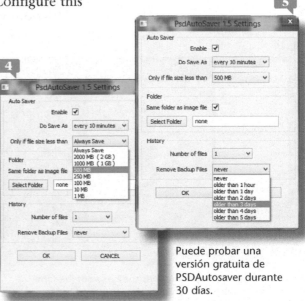

Puede probar una versión gratuita de PSDAutosaver durante 30 días.

Optimizing images for their publication

ONE OF THE MOST COMMON IMAGE FORMATS USED to display pictures on web pages or in multimedia formats is JPEG. Photoshop allows optimization of different images and formats and converts them to that format as well as establishing a quality for generated files that enables up to three JPEG files of different quality. Another widely used format for images is the Graphics Interchange Format or GIF. It is often used for indexed color images in HTML documents and preserves the transparency in indexed-color images without admitting alpha channels.

1. In this exercise you will learn how to optimize a GIF image by converting it to a JPEG file (JPEG is the compression standard format for continuous tone images). In order to do this, use an image in that format, you can use sample image **099.gif** if necessary. To begin, open the **File** menu and click on the **Save for Web** option. 🔽

2. The **Save for Web** box opens 🔽 and from this box you can display optimized images in different formats and with different attributes. From this box you can modify the tuning parameters while previewing the image and adjust them to best suit your needs. This time, you will convert the GIF im-

The **Save for Web** option opens the box with the same name from which you can optimize images by improving their quality and reducing their size in order to publish them online.

Enable the **Fit in View** option in the preview window so that you can see the entire image and the effects of the modifications.

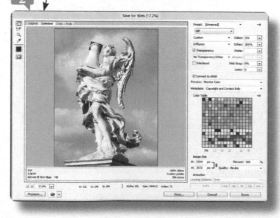

099

age to a JPEG image with high resolution. Click on the **Optimized File Format** field of the **Preset** section and select the **JPEG** format.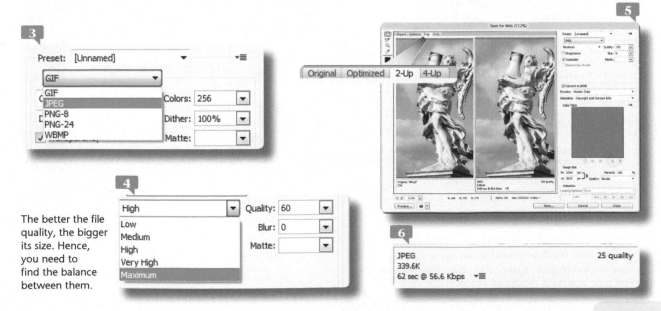

3. Click on the **Compression Quality** field and select the **Maximum** quality.

4. The **Quality** field now displays a value of 100. You can reduce this value manually to improve the compression. The higher the quality, the more details are retained by the compression algorithm. In order to see the original image and optimized one in the same window, click on the **2-Up** tab.

5. Under each image you can find its basic data. Since the image optimization is usually carried out in order to publish them on web pages or in multimedia, a part of this data is its estimated download time. Click on the **4-Up** tab.

6. Now all four files are displayed, starting with the original one and finishing with the one in lowest quality. Have a look at the differences in size, download speed, and quality among them. Redisplay the optimized image by clicking on the **Optimized** tab, press the button to the right of the download speed and select the option **Size/Download Time (2Mbps)**.

7. The download speed decreases dramatically. Press the **Save** button, see how the selected format for the optimization (JPEG) appears in the **Save Optimized As** box and save the optimized image.

7

Size/Download Time (9600 bps Modem)
Size/Download Time (14.4 Kbps Modem)
Size/Download Time (28.8 Kbps Modem)
✓ Size/Download Time (56.6 Kbps Modem/ISDN)
Size/Download Time (128 Kbps Dual ISDN)
Size/Download Time (256 Kbps Cable/DSL)
Size/Download Time (384 Kbps Cable/DSL)
Size/Download Time (512 Kbps Cable/DSL)
Size/Download Time (768 Kbps Cable/DSL)
Size/Download Time (1 Mbps Cable)
Size/Download Time (1.5 Mbps Cable/T1)
Size/Download Time (2 Mbps)

3

Preset: [Unnamed]

GIF

GIF
JPEG   Colors: 256
PNG-8
PNG-24   Dither: 100%
✓ WBMP   Matte:

4

The better the file
quality, the bigger
its size. Hence,
you need to
find the balance
between them.

High   Quality: 60
Low
Medium   Blur: 0
High
Very High   Matte:
Maximum

5

Original | Optimized | 2-Up | 4-Up

6

JPEG   25 quality
339.6K
62 sec @ 56.6 Kbps

Saving an image as a PDF

IN THE SAVE AS BOX YOU WILL FIND the PDF file type, which allows you to save RGB, Indexed, CMYK, Grayscale, Bitmap, Lab, and Duotones, in Portable Document Format (PDF). Photoshop CS6 also includes an automatic action in the Default Actions group of the Actions panel that automatically carries out this process.

1. To begin this exercise, open any picture in the Photoshop workspace, open the **File** menu and select the **Save As** option.

2. In the **Save As** box, open the **Format** field, select the **Photoshop PDF** option and click on the **Save** button.

3. Press the **OK** button in the information box that appears.

4. In the **Save Adobe PDF** box you need to establish the saving conditions for the document. You can use any of the presets that Photoshop offers or you can adjust the preferences to your needs. Click on the cursor button of the **Compatibility** option and select the adequate version for your case.

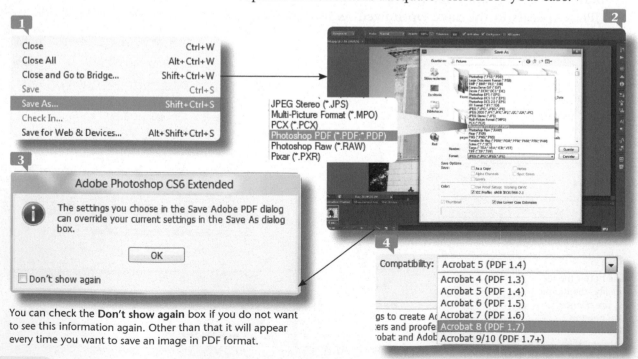

You can check the **Don't show again** box if you do not want to see this information again. Other than that it will appear every time you want to save an image in PDF format.

100

5. You can make other compression, output, and security adjustments in the **Summary** section, where you can see the general state of the settings. Enable the **View PDF After Saving the Overview** option in the **General** section so that the document opens in Acrobat after saving it in PDF format. 5

6. Press the **Save Preset** button to save the saving preferences you have carried out.

7. As you can see, the settings for PDF are stored by default in the Settings folder of Photoshop. This location can be changed if necessary. Assign a name for your custom setting and click on **Save.** 6

8. Press the **Save PDF** button to save the image.

9. A dialog box will inform you that the **Preserve Photoshop Editing Capabilities** option is not compatible with the earlier versions of the program. Click on the button **Yes** to continue. 7

10. As you have defined the saving options, Acrobat opens automatically (of course, this program needs to be installed on your computer) and displays the image converted to the PDF format, which can be shared with other users who do not have Photoshop. 8 To finish this exercise, close the PDF document by clicking on the Close button on the Title Bar.

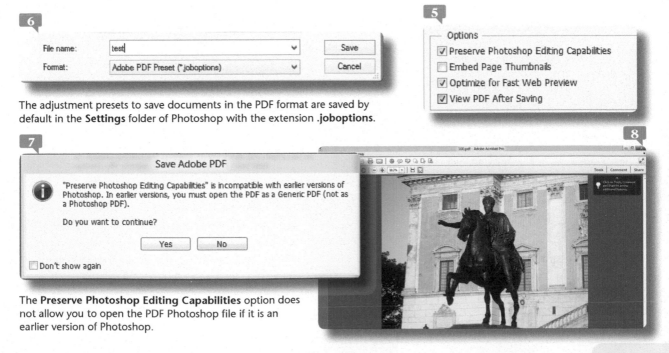

6

| File name: | test | ⌄ | Save |
| Format: | Adobe PDF Preset (*.joboptions) | ⌄ | Cancel |

The adjustment presets to save documents in the PDF format are saved by default in the **Settings** folder of Photoshop with the extension **.joboptions**.

5

Options
- ☑ Preserve Photoshop Editing Capabilities
- ☐ Embed Page Thumbnails
- ☑ Optimize for Fast Web Preview
- ☑ View PDF After Saving

7

Save Adobe PDF

"Preserve Photoshop Editing Capabilities" is incompatible with earlier versions of Photoshop. In earlier versions, you must open the PDF as a Generic PDF (not as a Photoshop PDF).

Do you want to continue?

[Yes]   [No]

☐ Don't show again

The **Preserve Photoshop Editing Capabilities** option does not allow you to open the PDF Photoshop file if it is an earlier version of Photoshop.

To continue learning...

IF THIS BOOK HAS FULFILLED YOUR EXPECTATIONS

This book is part of a collection that covers the most commonly used and known software in all professional areas.

All the books in the collection share the same aproach as the one you have just finished. So, if you would like to know more about other software packages, on the next page, you will find other books in this collection.

CREATING AND EDITING WEB SITES

If you are interested in creating and editing personal or professional websites, then *'Learning Dreamweaver CS6 with 100 practical exercises'* is perfect for you.

Dreamweaver is the industry standard for creating and editing web pages. This is the ideal software for web designers and developers to graphic designers. With this manual you will learn how to use it easily and conveniently.

With this book:

- You will meet the new grid-based CSS layout and work more comfortably with multiscreen options than before.
- You will make transitions based on CSS3 to apply smooth changes in the properties of the elements of a page.
- You will use creative web sources compatible with the Internet in Dreamweaver.
- You will apply the same elements in multiple CSS classes.

ILLUSTRATION

If you are more interested in illustrations, your ideal book would be *Learning Illustrator CS6 with 100 practical exercises.*

Illustrator is Adobe's vector-based drawing application that is an excellent tool for computer-aided design. Thanks to its incredible and powerful features, you can create original artwork by using it for pictures and drawings.

Within this book, you will learn to::

- Draw realistic brushstrokes with the new configurable bristle brushes
- Trace the most varied shapes
- Convert simple 2D drawings to incredible 3D objects
- Combine and edit shapes in order to obtain complex ones
- Draw realistic scenes in perspective

COLLECTION LEARNING... WITH 100 PRACTICAL EXERCISES

IN PREPARATION...

DESIGN AND ASSISTED CREATIVITY

- Dreamweaver CS6
- Flash CS6
- Illustrator CS6
- AutoCAD 2013

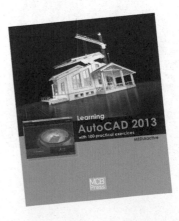